TAX SMART

THE TOUCHE ROSS GUIDE TO TOTAL TAX STRATEGY FOR 1988

Robert Wool is co-author of:

ALL YOU NEED TO KNOW ABOUT BANKS
ALL YOU NEED TO KNOW ABOUT THE IRS
HOW TO SURVIVE ON $50,000 TO $150,000 A YEAR

TAX SMART

THE TOUCHE ROSS GUIDE TO TOTAL TAX STRATEGY FOR 1988

How to Pay Less and Keep More Under the New Tax Law

ROBERT WOOL
with
TOUCHE ROSS

DELACORTE PRESS / NEW YORK

Published by
Delacorte Press
The Bantam Doubleday Dell Publishing Group, Inc.
1 Dag Hammarskjold Plaza
New York, New York 10017

Copyright © 1988 by Touche Ross & Co.

All rights reserved. No part of this book may be reproduced or transmitted in any form or by any means, electronic or mechanical, including photocopying, recording or by any information storage and retrieval system, without the written permission of the Publisher, except where permitted by law.

LIBRARY OF CONGRESS CATALOGING IN PUBLICATION DATA
Wool, Robert, 1934–
  Tax smart/Robert Wool and Touche Ross
    p. cm.
  Includes index.
  ISBN 0-385-29618-5
  1. Income tax—United States. 2. Tax planning—United States.
3. Income tax—Law and legislation—United States. I. Touche Ross
& Co. II. Title.
HJ4652.W73 1988
343.7305'2—dc 19
[347.30352]   87-27400
                                                              CIP

Manufactured in the United States of America

January 1988
10 9 8 7 6 5 4 3 2 1
BG

As *Tax Smart* went to press at the end of October 1987, Congress and the White House were discussing possible changes in the tax law. This book covers the law as it existed up to that date.
—R.W.

As always, for Bridget Potter,
my wife and finest editor,
and our daughters, Vanessa and Zoe,
helpers and small editors too

—R.W.

CONTENTS

Acknowledgments   xiii

Introduction   xv

1
The Impact of the Tax Reform Act of 1986:
The New Game   1
An overview of the many changes brought by the Tax Reform Act of 1986 as they affect individuals, and strategies to deal with them.

2
Tax-Smart Investing:
Life in Three Very Separate Baskets   35
How the new law changes *all* investment strategies by eliminating capital gains benefits, generally wiping out tax shelter techniques, and creating three separate kinds of income and losses.

3
Real Estate:
The Golden Days Turn Silver   54
Analysis of the far-reaching changes in real estate investing brought by the Tax Reform Act, once the quintessential tax-smart investment with its bundle of tax benefits and deductions, and a review of eight good strategies for successful real estate investing today.

4
Your Own Corporation:
A Shell Full of Tax Benefits   **80**

A full discussion of the many tax advantages of incorporating a small business, one area of great appeal that largely survived the Tax Reform Act.

5
Your Own Corporation:
Starting Small, with Big Plans   **102**

How to structure a new business, which the entrepreneur intends to expand and go public with, taking advantage of numerous tax benefits for his corporation, himself, and his family along the way.

6
Income Shifting:
Grand Slams, No-Hitters, and the Mighty Cliffords Strike Out   **125**

A review of the new law's disastrous consequences for income shifting from high-bracket parents to low-bracket children and a discussion of the strategies that survived.

7
Income Shifting:
Natalie's Quest—Something Big for an Average Person   **140**

Analysis of some 10 techniques for income shifting that still work and can serve the "average person."

8
Estate Planning:
Does One Size Fit All . . . Almost?   **157**

Overview of a critical, complex aspect of taxation that

could cost you tens or hundreds of thousands of dollars unless you understand basic techniques for cutting estate taxes. Discussion of the fundamental techniques and instruments to minimize those taxes.

**9
Estate Planning:**
Heavy Hitters 179
Continued discussions of ways to cut estate taxes, focused on some six strategies untouched by the new law.

**10
Retirement Plans:**
The Tax Law Still Has a Heart, Sort Of 191
A review of every major retirement plan, how each has been affected by the Tax Reform Act, and an analysis of ways an individual can construct a retirement plan for himself and his family.

Index 217

Acknowledgments

My thanks to a number of partners at Touche Ross.

To William Raby, Douglas Banks, John Connell, and Robert Zobel, who shared hours and hours of their time, as well as their tax smarts and experiences.

To Edwin Ruzinsky, who first recognized the possibilities of this book and who along with Michael Lux shepherded the book and coordinated the project within the firm.

To Gerald Padwe, Joseph Freimuth, and Farrell Rubenstein, whose support for the book was so useful.

To Eli Gerver, whose technical expertise was so important for the accuracy of the book.

Outside of Touche Ross, my thanks go to Jackie Farber, Editor-in-Chief of Delacorte Press, for her extremely helpful editorial guidance, and to her assistant, Donna Warkomski, for all her efficient juggling.

To Robert Parks, CPA, Technical Editor of *Tax Angles,* the newsletter I write, and to David Ackerman, CPA, for their assistance and encouragement.

And, finally, to George Wolper, a model CPA and uncle, from whom I inherited my passion for this subject.

—R.W.

Introduction

We all fear taxes.

On one level, our fears are pretty simple. We are afraid the IRS will catch us at something, like taking a friend to dinner and deducting it as a business expense, and hit us with fines and penalties and 20 lashes. (In the backs of our minds, of course, we all know that those folks can send us to jail too.)

On another level, things get more complex. We are afraid of the unknown—the fiercely dense and complicated tax law and the way it works.

We fear that we will make some innocent mistake out of our own ignorance, and it will cost us hundreds, thousands of dollars in taxes. (Who can keep track of even the deductions? So easy to overlook one. And what is this new monster, the AMT trap?)

Or, that out of this same ignorance we will not take advantage of a strategy, and the result will be the same—thousands in taxes paid needlessly.

All of these anxieties have been terribly intensified by the Tax Reform Act of 1986, which we have heard changes everything, and that simply makes everything more confusing and obscure than ever.

Of course, most of us have a safeguard. It's called "my accountant."

That trusted soul is not going to make any innocent mistake, we feel certain, overlook some deduction. He or she knows too much and is far too compulsive for that.

However, will he create for us one of those dazzling maneuvers we all hear about, those perfectly legal, breathtaking strategies that heavy hitters are always quietly applying to their million-dollar incomes, which cause all their taxes to vanish?

Of that, we are not so certain.

He may or may not know how to do a triple backflip off the high tower, but he is unlikely to share it with us. Because in addition to being compulsive, which we like, he seems to be genetically conservative, which we don't like so much.

One of the objectives of *Tax Smart* is to dispel many of your fears about taxes.

Another is to provide you with enough of an overview of taxes so that you can get more out of your accountant. After all, if you can't even ask the right questions, you can't expect him to give you the right answers.

However, *Tax Smart* will not make you into a CPA. It is not a tax course. And while it has been read and reread several times for accuracy, it is not all-inclusive. It is not a tax encyclopedia.

Nevertheless, it will provide you with a considerable amount of background and countless strategies, including backflips. The examples and cases around which the book is structured are composites drawn from the experiences of Touche Ross partners. They are plans that have worked for Touche Ross clients and might well work for you. Extrapolate from the book's examples and review it with your tax pro to see if it will apply to your particular tax condition.

Used that way, *Tax Smart* really could save you hundreds, thousands of dollars in taxes.

It could also help you relax a bit.

—Robert Wool

TAX SMART
THE TOUCHE ROSS GUIDE TO TOTAL TAX STRATEGY FOR 1988

1
The Impact of the Tax Reform Act of 1986: *The New Game*

They have changed all the rules.

That was what John R. Connell, partner of Touche Ross in Denver, was saying to himself as he read proposed legislation and Congressional Committee Reports all through the summer and fall of 1986.

And that was the plaintive cry he was hearing from his clients, as they gasped and struggled to make sense of the sweeping changes reported and misreported in their local newspapers and on their favorite TV news shows.

It was a complicated mess, but what they sensed was there was a whole new tax game, and it was going to be much tougher to play and win.

The last week in October, a few days after President Reagan had signed the Tax Reform Act of 1986, the most radical new tax law in more than 40 years, Connell, national director of Touche Ross's personal financial management services, received a call from one of his more sophisticated clients, Tom Fusco, a successful cable TV executive.

Fusco didn't even say hello. "John, what do we do now? I mean, this looks simply awful."

Quite obviously, Fusco had not bought the Administration's line and that of most of the new law's supporters that life would be wonderful now that tax rates were going to be drastically lowered. He had been reading between the lines and some of the small print as well. He knew that as a big earner with substantial investments, he was going to have to trade off a mountain of tax benefits for those lower rates. He knew he was going to have to scramble and come up with a whole new strategy.

Connell assured him that the sky had not fallen in, that there was still plenty they could do in the way of tax planning that could save him substantial tax dollars. They made an appointment for Fusco to come in the following week to review his entire financial and tax profile.

"It's so puzzling," Fusco said as they finished their conversation. He noted that a number of his favorite benefits, like capital gains, had been wiped out altogether. "What is life without capital gains?"

So much of the new stuff he simply could not grasp, entirely new creations like passive losses and gains, which were apparently now terribly important.

He was clear, however, about the drop in rates. It appeared that he would go from 50% in 1986 down to 38.5% for 1987, and then all the way down to 28%. "I don't know," he said, thinking aloud. "Maybe at 28%, I shouldn't even worry about taxes."

"You should worry," Connell replied. To begin with, he told him, he probably would never drop all the way down to 28%. There was a sneaky provision in the new law that would push big earners like him up to 33%. Add on another 5% he had to pay for local taxes, and he would be up around 38%.

That was certainly better than the more than 50% he was

now facing, Connell continued, but it was still going to be the single biggest expenditure he or any individual was going to have.

Furthermore, if they could figure ways to save him thousands of dollars on those taxes, wasn't that worth a worry?

Fusco got Connell's message. "See you next week, my friend."

Indeed the Tax Reform Act of 1986 was puzzling, not only to Fusco, but to Connell and his colleagues.

For months, as the committee reports from the House Ways and Means and the Senate Finance Committees and more detailed analyses came from the Touche Ross Washington office, Connell and his colleagues left the outside world. They disappeared into the hundreds of mind-numbing pages of proposed legislation, analysis, argument, and discussion.

The bill was first presented by the Treasury Department in November 1984. Treasury I, as it was called, was not taken all that seriously by professionals of the tax world because it was so sweeping in its proposed changes. Its inspiration was the "flat tax," in which there would be no deductions for anyone, no credits for anyone, all income would be taxed equally, and everyone would be taxed a flat percentage of income.

Almost two years later, the bill had evolved from Congress, pronounced dead more than once along the way, but amazingly emerging as a major overhaul of the tax law. In fact, after passing it, Congress changed the name of the entire tax law to the Internal Revenue Code of 1986.

The act itself was continually referred to by President Reagan as "tax simplification." It was anything but. In fact, all through 1987, Connell and others at Touche Ross were still figuring out the full meanings and ramifications of countless changes.

Fortunately, the Tax Reform Act (TRA) was structured to use 1987 as a transitional year, a time to begin the transition to new rules and to study the law itself.

Filing returns in the spring of 1987, Connell's clients like you and everyone else were operating under the old rules. It was the last chance for many to make a contribution to an IRA that would be deductible. It was the last chance, as Tom Fusco had sadly noted, for you to take advantage of the capital gains rules that allowed you to exclude 60% of any capital gain on a sale of an asset you had owned for more than six months.

Those and so many other profound changes would go into effect January 1, 1987, some earlier, but most people would not confront these changes, feel them until 1988. The returns you filed in the spring of 1987, in other words, were based on activities in 1986. The old rules still applied.

Only when it comes time to sit down with your own John Connell sometime between January 1, 1988, and April 15, 1988, the filing due date for personal federal income tax returns, not until then, will you fully realize the effect of the new law; not until then will you see the numbers. Hopefully, if you haven't already, you will begin then to revise your tax planning for the future.

As John Connell told Tom Fusco, and as this book will show you, while the rules in general have been changed, and many of your old favorites have been wiped out, the sky has not fallen. There are still countless tax-smart measures available to you, and they can still save you meaningful tax dollars.

Also, as Connell observed, for all the headlines about taxes being lowered, while that was true, income taxes remain the single biggest expenditure you will have this year.

Let's go beyond, far beyond the headlines.

From Connell's comfortable office on the 42nd floor of a downtown Denver office building, you can look out on the Rockies and, when the smog is right, even gaze upon Pike's Peak. An uplifting view, useful back in those first weeks after the law was passed.

Though the needs and the new plans to cope with them varied according to the client, there was with each of these meetings a preamble, an introductory overview that Connell orchestrated to give each client a sense of the major changes that would affect individual taxpayers.

They were of primary concern to everyone. For those clients who also owned or ran businesses, the discussion expanded, often with other Touche Ross partners dropping in to review their particular corporate specialties.

Tom Fusco came in to his meeting with a list of questions, most of which Connell had anticipated and made part of his general preamble. The special stuff dealt with deductions related to Fusco's work, and his passion, the stock market.

The law as advertised did lower everyone's tax rates, Connell told him, and it cut the number of brackets. In that sense, it might be said, there was tax simplification. But in no other.

Before the law, the top rate for individuals was 50%, and there were 15 different brackets.

For income earned in 1987, the top rate would be lowered to 38.5%, with five brackets.

And starting in 1988, and thereafter, the top rate would drop to 28%, with only one other bracket, 15%. That 28% could slide up to 33% for big earners, for couples showing taxable income of between $71,900 and $149,250 and for single people between $43,150 and $89,560.

Fusco and a lot of Connell's clients were going to end up being closer to 33% than 28%.

1987 Tax Rates

Taxable Income—Dollars

JOINT RETURN	SINGLE TAXPAYER	TAX RATE—%
Up to $3,000	Up to $1,800	11%
$3,001–$28,000	$1,800–$16,800	15%
$28,000–$45,000	$16,800–$27,000	28%
$45,000–$90,000	$27,000–$54,000	35%
Above $90,000	Above $54,000	38.5%

1988 (and after) Tax Rates

Taxable Income—Dollars

JOINT RETURN	SINGLE TAXPAYER	TAX RATE—%
Up to $29,750	Up to $17,850	15%
Over $29,750	Over $17,850	28%

More good news, Connell continued, with the standard deduction and personal exemptions. Both substantially increased.

The standard deduction is the amount of income the government says you can have tax-free. It was known as the *zero bracket amount,* and may be claimed by anyone who does not itemize his deductions. Since Fusco does itemize, he would not be helped here.

For 1987, a married couple filing jointly gets a standard deduction of $3760; single person, $2540.

For 1988, it goes up to $5000 and $3000.

You are entitled to a personal exemption on your return for yourself, for your spouse if you have one, and for any dependents you claim. For Fusco that would amount to four, himself and his wife with whom he files a joint return and their two children.

For 1987, Fusco will be able to deduct $1900 per exemption, and that will rise to $1950 in 1988 and $2000 in 1989, with the $2000 indexed for inflation beginning with 1990.

Once again, for big earners there will be something of a phaseout on this. Starting with taxable joint income over $149,250, they will be hit with an additional 5% of tax until the benefit from personal exemptions is wiped out. With a family of four this would mean at $194,050.

Fusco would not have to worry about the phaseout. Between his earnings at the cable company plus more from investments, and his wife's fees as a physical therapist, their gross income ranged from $175,000 to $200,000.

But once deductions were taken for the interest expense on the mortgages of both their principal residence and their second home, as well as all the rest of the deductions—local taxes, charitable contributions, the still-allowable portion of interest on consumer loans, and paper losses from tax shelters, especially from the investment in the Knoxville apartment complex, the Fuscos were well below the $149,250 level with their adjusted gross income (AGI), at least for 1987. Elimination of many of their deductions by the new law could leave them with a much higher AGI for 1988 and after.

All things considered, Connell told Fusco, you could say there is some good news, with the new lower rates and the higher standard deduction and personal exemption. But, all things closely considered, he still had deep reservations.

First of all, while it was true that taxes had been cut, many significant deductions and other benefits had been eliminated or cut back.

But perhaps more importantly, while everyone loved to see the rates go down, he didn't believe they were going to stay down. In his view, and that of so many of his colleagues, fairly soon, whether to pay off the national debt or for any number of political reasons, those rates would be pushed back up. (Significantly, in November of 1988, a new president will be elected.)

In light of all of these factors, Connell felt they should consider 1988 a strategic year for planning.

Nineteen eighty-eight might be the only year they will enjoy rates as low as 28%, and everyone has to take full advantage of that, he told Fusco. As much as possible, Fusco should try to pile income into 1988, whether it's deferred from 1987 or pulled from income that he would otherwise receive in 1989. He should try to get his 1989 bonus, for example, given to him in December of 1988.

As much as possible, he should attempt to defer deductions into 1989. If the rates did go up, those deductions would be worth that much more in 1989 and beyond.

It was good advice, which he offered all his clients. Focus all planning efforts on 1988.

No More Capital Gains Benefit

Connell shook his head and began the sad litany. "You mourned the passing of the capital gains rate," he said. "One of your favorites, you called it. A favorite for millions of people."

With that, if you owned an asset or property for more than six months it qualified for a long-term capital gain. If you sold it, you were allowed to exclude 60% of your gain from income taxes. You paid on only 40%, in other words, and that meant, even if you were in the highest bracket and paying at 50%, you were paying only a 20% tax on that gain (50% of 40%). And, of course, if you were in a lower bracket, say 40%, you paid proportionately less, only 16%.

It was a great incentive for investors, a great boon to building personal wealth. No more.

For 1987, when the top personal rate would be 38.5%,

you still got something of a break. Long-term capital gains would be taxed at a maximum of 28%.

But starting with 1988, these gains would be taxed just like any other income you earned, which could be 28% or up to 33%.

There was a ray of light, however, if you looked way down the tunnel, Connell observed. Though the big capital gains break was taken off the books, all of the language concerning capital gains was left in the tax code.

To Connell that was a clue that Congress was anticipating the possibility that they would have to give some special incentive back to investors, that they would have to give back some benefit on capital gains, some nice day in the future.

Pity the Poor IRAs

They've effectively wiped out the deductions for contributions to IRAs, Connell continued, which he found amazing. IRAs seemed sacred, the pension plan for everyman and everywoman.

With these you could contribute up to $2000 a year, $2250 if the contribution were for you and a nonworking spouse. Whatever you contributed up to those ceilings was deductible. And your investment fund was tax-free, in the sense that it earned money for you without any current taxes, a great advantage. It was taxed only when you drew it out, which did not have to be until age 70 1/2. For most people that meant the IRA would have many years to earn money on a tax-deferred basis.

Starting with 1987, if you or your spouse is an "active participant" in a qualified pension or profit-sharing plan where you work, the deductibility of your IRA contribution will be phased out as your joint adjusted gross income goes between $40,000 and $50,000 or between $25,000 and $35,000 for a single person.

In other words, only people who work at places that have no retirement plan, or don't qualify for one, or don't earn a great deal of money—below $40,000 jointly or $25,000 singly—will enjoy the old benefit. And chances are, Connell observed, people earning at that level aren't going to have much left over to put into an IRA after covering their basic living expenses.

If the new law excludes you, you may still make the $2000 contribution to an IRA, but it won't be deductible. It can still, however, earn for you on a tax-deferred basis.

"Will that make sense?" Connell asked rhetorically. Probably not, he thought. You'll have to compare that with other tax-deferred or, even better, tax-free possibilities, like municipal bonds, municipal bond mutual funds, municipal bond trust funds. The problem for a lot of people with IRAs is that they won't feel very comfortable doing it. They don't understand the muni market, which can be tricky.

Connell shook his head again. Fusco would survive, even though it would cost him and his wife those nice $2000 deductions, but it would hurt a lot of people.

Say Good-bye to Interest Deductions

Last year, Connell reminded Fusco, he and his wife ran up interest charges of more than $4000, not counting the mortgage interest paid on his homes.

It was the usual stuff, from credit cards and the cost of carrying two automobiles, a chunk of money though hardly excessive for their income, and completely typical of the American way of living.

All of that $4000 was deductible. No more.

Now consumer interest, as that is called, will no longer be deductible, to be phased out over four years. With consumer interest you incur in 1987, you may deduct 65%. In 1988, 40%. In 1989, 20%. In 1990, 10%, and nothing thereafter.

Nor will anything be allowed any longer for local sales taxes. With Fusco as with everyone, that deduction varied from year to year depending on the amount of major purchases made during a year. But around Denver, with a sales tax of more than 7%, he would normally have a deduction of about $885, and in 1986, when he bought a new Volvo for $22,000, the figure rose to $2450.

All gone. And no phaseout grace period either. After December 31, 1986, nothing.

Fusco was disturbed. Losing $8000, $9000 in deductions just like that was really going to hurt.

"It won't," Connell told him. "I've got a plan, and it's all quite legal. It's called 'charity begins at home.'"

The new law, he explained, says you may refinance or otherwise borrow against your principal residence and/or second home up to the amount you paid for it plus improvements, what is technically your "basis," and all of the interest you pay on that amount will be completely deductible, practically no matter what you do with the funds.

In Fusco's case, he had paid $125,000 for the house some years earlier, and it needed a lot of work. Discounting cosmetic paint jobs and minor repairs, he had put some $40,000 into structural changes in the house of the sort that would qualify as improvements: a new kitchen, an attic converted into a bedroom, a new bathroom installed on the main floor, the chimney and fireplace rebricked.

That meant he could refinance up to $165,000 ($125,000 cost plus $40,000 improvements) and deduct all the interest.

They estimated that Fusco owed about $30,000 for cars

and other loans that fell under "consumer interest." All of that would be paid off with a portion of the new mortgage. That way Fusco would not lose a penny of the interest deduction on that $30,000.

He also owed $75,000 on his original mortgage, and his bank would want that paid off if there were refinancing. So they would divide the plan into two parts.

Fusco would take a new mortgage for $105,000 to pay off the $30,000 in consumer debts and the $75,000 balance on the first mortgage.

In addition, Connell recommended that he get one of those new lines of credit secured by the balance in his home that all the banks are pushing these days for the $60,000 remaining in his basis.

Though banks charge a higher rate of interest for that, he could draw against it if and when he wanted to use it for some purchase and again protect the interest deduction. Otherwise, he would buy the VCR, dishwasher, or whatever, charge it, and lose the deduction on all the interest connected with it. If it turned out that that wasn't enough, Connell told him, he could apply the same refinancing strategy with his second home.

Fusco was delighted with the prospect of salvaging thousands of dollars in deductions, but he had a critical question. How much of a burden would he have with the mortgage payments on $165,000?

Connell assured him he could handle it painlessly. First of all, he wouldn't start with the whole amount. Only $105,000. At today's rates, that would be only about $925 a month. He could afford that easily.

In fact, he could also afford the payments on $165,000. Undoubtedly, there would be an awful lot of people who would try to use this maneuver, Connell speculated, who would find themselves overextended, perhaps even endanger their homes. But that was not going to be the case with Fusco.

Fusco thought for a moment, then hesitantly offered a plan of his own. If he could afford to be extended to $165,000, why not do it? Why not take the whole amount and put the balance right into the market?

In fact, Connell told him, that might help them deal with another problem, the new limits on the deductibility of investment interest. Fusco loved the market, and it was only out of respect for Connell that he developed the patience to wait more than six months on most of his investments. Like most players with a high risk threshold, he traded on margin, the maximum allowed. Recently, this has been 50%.

The interest on that margin, which was after all money the brokerage house was lending him, was deductible under the old law up to the amount of net investment income plus $10,000. Every year with Fusco, that amounted to serious amounts, another big deduction. For 1986, it was $3000.

The new law cut out the extra $10,000. Such interest would be deductible up to the amount of net investment income, period.

However, if he took a portion of his new mortgage and invested it, all of the interest on that portion as with all the rest of the new mortgage loan would be completely deductible.

Miscellaneous Itemized Deductions

Connell warned him that they would have to try to change the way they handled a number of business-related deductions. In the past, Fusco incurred a certain amount of expenses in connection with his business that were not reimbursed by his company and he was expected to cover himself.

These started with special travel expenses. Though his corporate office was in Denver, as were several other cable companies, as senior vice president in charge of sales and marketing Fusco had to travel a lot, and he always went first class or business class. Not only did he actually meet people and improve his chances of meeting people who developed into customers in those classes, but he didn't like to fly. The additional space and comfort were worth the extra money to him. He could arrive at his business destination and be less of a nervous wreck. Fusco paid the difference, and it was deductible.

He also belonged to a health club, which he used more than half the time for business. Often he'd play a game of racquetball with a customer, take a swim, and when they sat down for lunch or dinner, they'd talk business.

Connell was insistent that he keep careful records of when he used the club for business as opposed to personal, the names of clients, amounts charged to the account.

It was all legitimate as business expense, but in his deal with his company, he was to cover such expenses, so he did and deducted it.

His wife subscribed to a number of professional publications for her work, and they were also legitimate miscellaneous itemized deductions.

So were the courses she took to keep up with developments in the physical therapy field.

While all of these now would still be deductible items, there was a new 2% floor. They would have to add up all the items in this miscellaneous category, and only the amount that exceeded 2% of their adjusted gross income would be deductible.

For the Fuscos, that was going to be a very high figure. If their AGI, for example, was $125,000, their miscellaneous items would have to amount to more than $2500 before a penny could be deducted.

And then, only the amount exceeding $2500 counted. If the total was $3000, they could deduct $500 only. If the total was $2000, they could deduct nothing.

Some of Connell's clients were going to try bunching these miscellaneous deductions, even running the risk of being slightly delinquent in paying bills, so they could accumulate enough in one year to beat the 2% floor.

But that still would not help Fusco with the first $2500, and besides, a number of his miscellaneous deductions could not be stalled several months. His health club would throw him out if he fell that far behind in his payments.

Connell had another possibility. Fusco had to convince his company to pay for as much of this as possible. If they wouldn't do it as a bonus to him, perhaps he could work out a plan where he took less salary in exchange for a reimbursement. They reimburse him all the legitimate business expenses that he had been taking as miscellaneous itemized deductions, and he takes that much less in salary.

He might have to declare the reimbursement as income, but the law allows him to deduct his business expenses fully against that income. He would avoid the 2% floor and not lose that part of his deduction.

New Medical Limits

When it came to medical expenses that had not been reimbursed by some insurance program, the old law had a floor of 5%.

It worked like the floor for miscellaneous items. You could deduct only the amount that exceeded 5% of your AGI. That was an extremely high figure for most people. For the Fuscos, it might mean $6250.

Fortunately, their family had not suffered the kinds of illnesses that pushed their medical expenses so high they were left with substantial amounts not covered by their insurance.

From now on, should they encounter such disasters, it would be even tougher for them to deduct any of their excessive expenses. The floor was being raised to 7.5%.

There was one piece of relief for such expenses, however, that Connell mentioned as something they should both keep in the backs of their minds in case the emergency arose.

It was "charity begins at home" again. In addition to using the principal residence and second home as sources of capital with deductible interest as he had already described, the new law extended that principle to medical and educational expenses.

For these, you could exceed the other limits. You could go above your basis, what you paid for the house plus improvements, up to the fair market value of your house. Refinance as needed to pay the medical bills, to cover tuition and related costs, and deduct all the interest.

So, he advised, if you get hit with medical bills that aren't covered by insurance, pay them through the home. Write a check off the home credit line the bank gives you. Or, if that's used up, get an additional mortgage from the bank.

Fusco's children were still years away from college, and he had bought zero coupon bonds for them, at Connell's advice some years earlier. These were scheduled to mature when the children entered college. However, if costs at that time were even higher than they had anticipated, the extra money could come from his homes.

Presently, they attended public schools. But if Fusco and his wife decided to put them into private schools, those tuition and other expenses could be financed through the additional home mortgage up to its fair market value.

One other possibility, Connell noted, with those zero

coupon funds: they could be used for investment purposes instead of paying the colleges. And the colleges could be paid by refinancing the homes.

It was another way when the time came that Fusco could get his hands on a substantial amount of cash to invest, or use as he pleased, and still enjoy the big interest deduction that would come from the new loan.

There was a bunch of deductions eliminated by the new law, Connell went on, that didn't amount to much, except for one, the two-earner deduction.

This was simply hard-hearted of Congress in Connell's view. The "marriage penalty" deduction, as it was called, was a recognition by Congress that two married people who worked could end up paying more in taxes than they would if they were two people with the same incomes filing as single people. Unfair, Congress said in 1981, and allowed a compensating deduction with a $3000 ceiling.

The Fuscos as two working marrieds always took advantage of the deduction. Now, it would be gone. Congress maintained that by lowering the tax rates there would be sufficient fairness for everyone.

In the same spirit, they repealed the $50 credit, $100 jointly, for political contributions.

And took away the exclusion of $100 or $200 jointly of dividend income.

Even Connell had to allow that those two were losses everyone would survive.

Income Averaging

And then there was one rule that was repealed that didn't make a great deal of difference most of the time, but every once in a while, it could save your life.

In Fusco's case, he had had one year in which he had changed jobs, practically doubled his salary, and had two or three mining stocks that soared. In addition to his vastly increased compensation, he made over $100,000 in the market alone that year.

For that year, Connell did income averaging. He took Fusco's extraordinary income figure for that year, averaged it with the three years that went before—when his salary was much lower.

As a result, instead of having to pay income taxes based on the one spectacular year alone, Fusco was able to average out income over the four years and save tens of thousands of dollars. However, income averaging had been wiped out, and if Fusco were to have another incredible year, it would have to stand on its own.

Office at Home

Fusco's job did require him to do a great deal of work at home. The old and new laws allowed him to deduct certain expenses connected with the office he maintained for that purpose, provided he met a number of requirements, among them that the space was used for his office and only for that, that he used it to meet customers, and that it was maintained for the convenience of his employer.

On that basis, a share of the heating bill for the house—the amount equal to the office's proportionate space in the entire house—was deductible. Same for electric bills. If Fusco were renting the house, the same portion could be deducted from the rent. And he deducted a proportionate amount for depreciation each year. (There were other possible deductions—for example, a share of the mortgage interest expense, local real estate taxes—but Fusco deducted those fully as an individual anyway. For other Connell clients who had income-producing free-lance businesses they were running from offices in their homes, those deductions were quite meaningful. They drastically cut down the amount of taxable income the sideline business ended up with.)

Still, this was a deduction the IRS regularly tried to knock out. It was the same for all of Connell's clients who claimed it, whether they used it as Fusco did to supplement their principal office or they used it for a second free-lance business. If they got audited, there was always a battle over the office in the home.

Connell didn't mind the battles, but a couple of years ago he thought he discovered a strategy that would end them. An accountant had an office built into his home. Though he had an office in his firm, he contended that because of phone calls, people continually popping in and out of his office, he could not do any work that required sustained quiet and concentration. That could be done only at his office at home.

He then leased the office at home to his firm. They paid him rent, which he declared as income, against which he took every allowable deduction for such business space.

The IRS naturally went after him, but the courts upheld him. And a new strategy was born.

Connell could remember the morning he read the case and called Fusco with the suggestion that he work out precisely the same arrangement with his own firm. He would have his office at home and be done with the IRS audit battles.

Fusco's firm agreed. The rent wasn't much, but it allowed him to cover expenses on the space, and one washed out the other. And perhaps just as meaningful, Connell and Fusco shared the pleasure of having beaten the IRS.

The new law brought an end to such small joys. Because the IRS complained so loudly, Congress specifically disallowed home office deductions where employers rented the space from the employee.

Connell had to smile as he told Fusco about "hobby losses," which would also now be tougher to write off. After all, he protested, if a man wants to try to be a farmer in addition to being a business executive, he ought to have a shot at it. It's a free country.

Fusco was quick to remind him that that was one maneuver he never tried.

Connell nodded. He wasn't thinking of Fusco but a number of his oil clients with big farms all over the Southwest. It used to be you were supposed to show a profit in two out of five consecutive years, or the IRS called it a hobby, not a business. Big difference in deductions. Now, just to be mean, they changed it to three years out of five.

If you were raising horses, the rule remained unchanged, two years out of seven. A small concession that wouldn't amount to much anyway because of passive losses.

All those clients with all those perfectly legitimate losses coming from their horse farms, which for years had been extremely handy when Connell applied them against income from salaries and investments, all those lovely losses would now be passive and could be applied against passive income only (as we'll see in the next chapter).

Hobby losses and horse farms were at least problems that Fusco would not have. But there was another, potential problem looming out there, something they didn't have to worry much about in the past, but which now they'd have to keep a close watch on, the alternative minimum tax (AMT).

Expanded AMT trap

The alternative minimum tax is nothing new, Connell explained. There's been a minimum tax since 1969 and more or less in its present form since 1978. Essentially it is Congress's way of forcing everyone to pay some taxes. True, there were still people, some very-high-income people who got around it, but not many, and now there will be even fewer.

The AMT is, as the name suggests, an alternative computation of your taxes.

The first time around, you figure out your regular taxes taking every possible deduction and credit you're entitled to.

With the AMT, you take your regular taxable income and add back into your computation many of those same deductions and credits. They were called *preference items* and included things like the 60% of capital gains that you excluded. If you elected accelerated depreciation rather than straight-line on rental property (which we'll consider in Chapter 3), the difference was added back into your figures. Deductions that used to be prevalent with tax shelters, like mining exploration and development costs and intangible drilling costs from oil investments, were also preference items and still are.

You redo your taxes with those addbacks, factor in an exemption of $40,000 for married filing jointly, $30,000 for singles, and figure out the tax at 20%, now 21%. (The exemption gets phased out at the highest levels, reduced by 25% for AMT income [AMTI] over $150,000 for married couples filing jointly, disappearing completely at $310,000 of AMTI.)

If the dollar amount of the AMT is higher than that of

your regular tax computation with all of its deductions, you pay the AMT. If the regular is higher, you pay that.

For many big earners who were also big investors in tax-advantaged investments, this meant that despite all their carefully planned deductions—especially from capital gains and tax shelters—they still had to pay taxes at the 20% rate. Which was still better than paying at a 50% rate, if not as good as paying zero or next to it.

Now the new law has expanded the AMT base, adding preference items and "adjustment" items and raising the rate to 21%.

Obviously, with capital gains benefits eliminated, that is no longer part of the AMT calculation. But you will have to add back passive activity net losses you deduct. And any tax-exempt interest on certain private activity bonds will be swept back into the AMT calculation.

The home interest deductions on your principal residence and second homes could be affected. As noted on your regular tax, one of the few major deductions still in good shape is this one, allowing you to deduct all the interest on a refinanced mortgage up to the amount you paid for the house plus improvements. The AMT allows a deduction only for the amount of the immediately prior balance of your mortgage. Refinance for more than your prior balance, and it's not allowed.

Also, for your regular tax, you enjoy the interest deduction pretty much no matter what you do with the mortgage funds. But with the AMT, you get a deduction only if the proceeds are used for acquiring, constructing, or substantially rehabilitating the property being mortgaged.

One new AMT provision could severely affect charitable institutions. Before, if you gave dear old Dartmouth a painting worth $10,000 in the marketplace, which you had bought some years before for $5000, there was no tax for you on the appreciation. You had a capital gain of $5000 without any tax on it, yet you received a charitable deduction for the full $10,000. Further, there was no effect so far as the AMT went. You didn't have to add back any of that $5000.

The Tax Reform Act changes that. While you will still not be taxed on the appreciation, you now have to add back the appreciation when you figure your AMT.

But the biggest change so far as the AMT is concerned and the one that will force us to watch it closely for the first time, Connell told Fusco, is that it now is at a rate very close to what the top rate is intended to be.

The AMT will be 21%. The top rate for 1988 is to drop to 28-33%. When the top rate was 50% and AMT 20%, you might be able to get your income tax figure down to an effective rate of, say, 30%, with all your deductions and credits. So, the AMT didn't affect that many taxpayers. Only the very big earners and investors.

Now, however, it won't be that difficult to lower your income tax bill to an amount that will activate the AMT.

Not only will that mean that you'll end up paying more taxes than you had planned for, but it will greatly diminish the value of a number of the investments you make.

For example, suppose you make an investment in real estate, even if it is now a passive activity, and you figure that you can make use of the losses it throws off, and they will be worth 28 cents or 33 cents on the dollar to you. Ten thousand dollars in losses will save you $2800-$3300. That is not the $5000 it used to be, but still you'd rather have the $2800-$3300 in your pocket than in an IRS account.

However, if it turns out that you trigger the AMT, you will have to pay taxes on 21% of that 28% saving, so all you've saved on the deal is 7%, $700.

Multiply this by two or three such AMT blows, and you have large, painful holes in your entire tax plan.

Fusco listened to Connell's explanation and then raised a

question that gets to the heart of the AMT dilemma for any taxpayer: How in the world could he know where he stood in relation to the AMT at any given point? If he were thinking of an investment, how could he know whether it would drop him into the trap?

The truth is, Connell told him, he really couldn't. Connell was not trying to create business, but only an accountant or someone who spends nearly all his time monitoring such a thing was going to be able to tell. The rules for it and the calculations are so complex, Connell thought it was practically unconstitutional, cruel and unusual punishment.

He would keep tabs. Then anytime Fusco was planning an investment or a charitable contribution with an appreciated property, anything that might conceivably trigger an AMT consequence, Fusco would have to check with him, and he'd update the AMT computation.

Then they'd decide what strategy was best.

It might be, for example, that a charitable gift would put him into AMT. Maybe they would postpone the gift to next year or divide it between two years.

If they could see an AMT year clearly developing, they might try to accelerate income into that year and have it taxed at 21%, rather than 33% as it might otherwise be taxed in a non-AMT year.

Similarly, for such a year they might try to defer deductions, because they would be worth only 21% in an AMT year, as opposed to 33% in a non-AMT year.

They would simply have to take it step by step, carefully, very carefully, Connell told him.

What Connell was going through with Fusco and dozens of his other clients was being played out in various forms in Touche Ross offices around the country.

In Miami, Robert Zobel, who like Connell did a great deal of personal financial planning and specialized in income shifting and estate planning, ministered to a flock of dazed, almost shell-shocked clients.

"They dropped a bomb on us, an atom bomb," said one of his clients, reviewing the effects of changes in the laws that once allowed him to use Clifford trusts and other instruments to shift income to his children with little or no tax consequence. "There's nothing left."

"Damaging," Zobel told him, "but not a complete wipeout" (as we'll see in Chapter 6, "Income Shifting: Grand Slams, No-Hitters, and the Mighty Cliffords Strike Out," and in Chapter 7, "Income Shifting: Natalie's Quest —Something Big for an Average Person").

The sweeping changes and new limitations on income shifting affected the options available with estate planning. Elimination of Clifford trusts, for example, and taxing unearned income for children under age 14 at their parents' rate made it much more difficult for Zobel's clients to shift assets from their estates and cut down the amount of potential estate tax liability.

But the range of possibilities was still great, and certainly the need to plan was as essential as ever. (See Chapter 8, "Estate Planning: Does One Size Fit All . . . Almost?" and Chapter 9, "Estate Planning: Heavy Hitters.")

In Phoenix, William Raby, Senior Partner of the firm, with specialties in guiding small businesses and devising retirement plans, had his share of worried and perplexed clients. For the first time since the Sixteenth Amendment was ratified in 1913 and individuals were taxed by the federal government, the corporate income tax rate would now be higher than the personal income tax rate.

For many of Raby's clients this meant reviewing the way they did business. Would it now be more beneficial to convert their regular C corporations to S corporations? With the lower personal rates, might they be better off passing all of their corporate earnings through to themselves and other stockholders, rather than retaining the earnings in the corporation as much as the law allowed?

Most of them, it turned out, were better off the way they were.

While the Tax Reform Act brought a number of changes to corporations, it did not eliminate many of the significant tax benefits available to people who are able to work within a corporate structure, whether they are doctors and other professionals or entrepreneurs starting new businesses. (See Chapter 4, "Your Own Corporation: A Shell Full of Tax Benefits," and Chapter 5, "Your Own Corporation: Starting Small, with Big Plans.")

Retirement planning certainly was affected by the new law, and Raby, Connell, and others had to explain to their clients that for most of them IRA deductions were a thing of the past, and they could no longer put up to $30,000 into their 401(k) plans. The new limit was $7000, and when they went to draw the money out of such qualified retirement plans, they would get less of a tax break, with 10-year averaging cut to five-year averaging.

What had not changed were the basic questions anyone looking ahead asked himself: When am I going to retire? How much am I going to need to live the way I'm accustomed to living? Where's the money going to come from? (See Chapter 10, "Retirement Plans: The Tax Law Still Has a Heart, Sort Of.")

For all the changes wrought by the Tax Reform Act of 1986, none seemed to strike and confuse more Touche Ross clients than those affecting investing in general and real estate in particular.

Real estate had been something of a promised land for investors. All kinds of deductions were passed along to them from the activities they invested in, deductions for mortgage interest being paid by their projects, for real estate taxes, for any number of other business expenses, and most especially for depreciation.

The result was an investment that, if made wisely, could bring substantial paper losses every year, perhaps two or three times the cash invested, and those paper losses could be applied against real income from salary and other sources, wiping out the income for tax purposes. All those dollars that otherwise would go to the government went right into the investor's pocket.

In addition, in five to 10 years, when the property was sold, there would presumably be more good news for the investor, a gain to be realized on the sale.

But as Douglas Banks, Touche Ross's National Director of Real Estate in Washington, D.C., was explaining to his clients, the golden days were over. (See Chapter 3, "Real Estate: The Golden Days Turn Silver.")

Congress had created three kinds of income: active, which includes areas where the taxpayer "materially participates," such as his regular job, which pays him a salary; portfolio, typically the income from investments in stocks and bonds; and an entirely new animal, passive, which among other distinctions resulted from activities in which the taxpayer did not materially participate.

So far as real estate and investments are concerned, all rental properties are categorized as passive, and so are all limited partnerships, which is the form of the traditional real estate syndicate into which a client invested.

And, if these investments yield any losses, on paper or in reality, those losses may be applied against passive income only, not against nonpassive income like salaries as in the old days. Now if you have a loss from a rental property, you may apply that against income from some other passive activity, real estate or otherwise.

In other words, little or no more sheltering income as before.

These changes, plus the elimination of the capital gains benefits, profoundly affected not only real estate but all other kinds of investing as well, as we will see in the next chapter.

Checklist: Chapter 1

Tax-smart strategies and perspectives for you to consider and discuss with your tax professional:

1. The Tax Reform Act of 1986 lowers the tax rates for individuals and cuts the number of tax brackets.

For income earned in 1987, the top rate drops from 50% to 38.5%. Instead of 15 brackets, there will be only five.

In 1988 and thereafter, the top rate goes down to 28%, with only one other bracket, 15%.

The 28%, however, slides upward to 33% for big earners, for couples showing taxable income of between $71,900 and $149,250 and for single people between $43,150 and $89,560.

Of course, local and state taxes must be figured on top of those federal amounts.

And while the rates were lowered, a vast number of deductions and credits were eliminated or limited (see below).

Alas, taxes remain everyone's single biggest expenditure.

2. Standard deductions and personal exemptions are increased under the new law.

The standard deduction is the amount of income the law allows you to have tax-free. You may claim it, if you do not itemize.

For the year 1987 a married couple filing jointly is entitled to a standard deduction of $3760; a single person, $2540.

For 1988, it goes up to $5000 and $3000.

You take a personal exemption for yourself, your spouse if you file jointly, and any dependents you legitimately claim.

For 1987 each personal exemption will be $1900, and that rises to $1950 in 1988 and $2000 in 1989.

There is a phaseout on personal exemptions for big earners. Starting with taxable joint income over $149,250, they will be hit with an additional 5% of tax until the benefit from personal exemptions is wiped out.

3. In all your tax planning, factor in the possibility that tax rates will not stay as low as presently advertised. They may drop from 38.5% to 28% for 1988, but they may well rise back up. Pressures on Congress to cut the federal deficit and other political factors could force the rise.

That could make 1988 a key year. Accelerate income into 1988 to take advantage of the low rates before they are pushed up. Defer deductions into 1989, when the rates might be higher, so your deductions will be worth that much more.

4. The capital gains exclusion is eliminated. You were allowed to exclude 60% of your gain on the sale of an asset you had owned for more than six months.

That meant you paid at the rate of only 20% if you were in the highest bracket, 50%, and only 16% if you were in the 40% bracket.

Such a benefit affected investment philosophy generally, since it was usually well worth waiting more than six months before selling a stock, a piece of property.

Its elimination means a new tax-smart approach to investing, as we'll see in Chapter 2.

Tax professionals note and take hope in the fact that Congress decided to keep the capital gains language in the tax code, even though the exclusion was wiped out. A sign, perhaps, that the benefit might be restored, if Congress decides that, without that incentive, taxpayers are limiting their investments to the point where the economy is suffering.

5. You may no longer take a full deduction for your IRA contribution if you or your spouse, assuming joint filing, has a retirement plan available at work and your joint adjusted gross income goes between $40,000 and $50,000 or between $25,000 and $35,000 for a single person.

You may still deposit up to $2000 in your IRA, even if you don't get the deduction, and your IRA will continue to earn for you on a tax-deferred basis over the years. You are not taxed on that until you take the money out.

If you do not qualify for the deduction, compare existing tax-deferred or tax-free alternative investments like municipal bonds or municipal bond mutual or trust funds before you make the IRA contribution.

6. Interest on consumer credit is no longer deductible under the Tax Reform Act. This includes interest from credit cards, on loans to pay for cars and major appliances, etc.

The law allows you to deduct 65% of such interest paid in 1987, 40% in 1988, 20% in 1989, 10% in 1990, and nothing thereafter.

Local sales taxes are also wiped out as a deduction, with no phaseout grace period.

7. Refinance your principal residence and possibly second home as well.

The new law says you may refinance on those two homes, principal and second, up to the amount you paid for the house plus improvements and deduct all the interest on that new mortgage or mortgages.

If you have substantial consumer debts outstanding, a bank loan on a car for example, since the interest on those loans will no longer be fully deductible, refinance your home and pay off the car loan. All the interest then will be deductible.

You may use the money from refinancing to invest as well and still enjoy the full interest deduction.

That may help you with another interest change in the law—investment interest.

Previously, you could deduct interest on money you borrowed for investment purposes up to the amount of your net investment income *plus* $10,000. If you were a heavy investor, that was a significant deduction for you.

Now you are limited to a deduction on interest up to the amount of your net investment income.

However, the funds you use for investments that come from a new mortgage will still bring you a complete deduction on the interest.

8. Two percent floor on miscellaneous deductions. These include business and professional books and journals you subscribe to, courses you take to improve your skills in your existing job, business expenses the company does not reimburse you for.

Now you may deduct only the amount that exceeds 2% of your adjusted gross income. So, if you show an AGI of $100,000, the miscellaneous expenses must be more than $2000 before you may deduct a penny. If they amount to, say, $1700, you lose the entire deduction. If they amount to, say, $2200, you may deduct only $200, the amount that exceeds the 2% floor.

It might be possible for you to bunch these deductions, hold off paying them in one year, double them up in the next. You will still lose out on the amount below the 2% floor, but bunched together, they might exceed 2%, and you would at least salvage the excess amount as a deduction.

Even better, try to get your company to cover as many of these expenses as possible. You will have to work out the numbers, but you might be better off if you took proportionately less salary in exchange for their paying these expenses directly or reimbursing you. You would have to declare the reimbursement as additional income, but the law allows you to deduct business expenses fully against such income. That way you would avoid the 2% floor.

9. Floor on medical expenses increases from 5% to 7.5%. Only unreimbursed medical expenses that exceed 7.5% of your AGI will be deductible starting with 1987.

That is a terribly high amount. On $100,000 of AGI, only the amount over $7500 will be deductible, and everything below it lost.

10. Special deductions for medical and educational expenses. Over and above the refinancing allowed on your principal residence and second home—cost plus improvements—the new law will permit you to extend your mortgage to the fair market value of your home to pay for medical expenses or educational expenses and, most importantly, deduct all the interest on those extended loans.

Most people have insurance to cover the great part of their medical expenses, but if you exceed the coverage, consider paying through your home mortgage.

You may also replace capital for medical and educational expenses through a home refinancing. So, if you pay $10,000 for a prep school or college expense for your child, you may in effect repay yourself that $10,000 from the refinancing and have the money for investment or other purposes.

11. No more two-earner deduction, credit for political contributions, or exclusion for dividends. No more income averaging.

Married people who work were entitled to a deduction of up to $3000, so they wouldn't be penalized just for being married. As singles with the same incomes, their taxes would be lower. The new law eliminates the compensating deduction.

The Impact of the Tax Reform Act of 1986

Ditto for the small credit, $50 or $100 jointly, for political contributions.

Ditto for the exclusion of $100 or $200 of dividend income.

Income averaging gave you a huge break if you had one year when you earned considerably more than normal for yourself. You were then allowed to average it with the three years that preceded the big year and pay the tax based on that average. The tax savings could be dramatic.

All gone. The IRS will now share fully in the pleasure of a whopping big year.

12. Office at home rules tightened. The new law specifically bars the office at home deductions for a bold new strategy conceived by an accountant: his firm rented space in his home from him that he used for an office. It was a way around the stringent restrictions for these deductions. No more.

13. Expanded AMT trap. The alternative minimum tax is a way to force all taxpayers to pay some tax. Extremely complex, it basically requires you to do a second, alternative tax computation after completing your regular computation.

In the AMT, you include or add back a number of deductions called *preference items* you are allowed in the regular computation; e.g., capital gains exclusion (before the change), depreciation, mining exploration and development costs, intangible drilling costs from oil investments.

With the preferences added back, you recalculate, take the allowed exemption of $40,000 for married filing jointly, $30,000 for singles, then figure out the tax at 20% under the old law, 21% under the new.

If the dollar amount of the AMT amounts to more than that of your regular tax calculation with all its deductions and credits, you pay the AMT. If the regular is higher, you stick with that.

Previously, the AMT was a worry for very big investors only. Now, however, the number of preferences has been expanded and "adjustment" items added, so more taxpayers will be affected.

And, with the new rates, the regular and the AMT rates are quite close, theoretically at 28% and 21%. When they were 50% and 20%, there was such a spread that only people with extremely heavy deductions hit the AMT. Otherwise, they might reduce their taxes by a goodly amount but still be higher than AMT.

But now it won't be that difficult to lower your tax bill to the level where you trigger the AMT.

If that happens, then investments on which you anticipated a tax saving of, say, 28%, or $2800 on every $10,000 of paper losses, will now be reduced to only a 7% saving, the difference between your anticipated 28% regular rate and the 21% AMT rate.

On that basis, an investment might not be worth making in the first place, assuming you know you are going to be paying AMT.

Unfortunately, monitoring where you stand in relation to the AMT is so complicated, it is best done by your tax professional and done before you make any major investment or tax-sensitive financial move.

Then, together you might decide, for example, if a charitable contribution is going to trigger the AMT, you might delay the contribution for a year or divide it between this year and next.

Or, if you see an inevitable AMT year developing, attempt to accelerate income into that year and have it taxed at 21% rather than 33%.

Or, conversely, defer deductions in such a year, since they would be worth only 21%, rather than 33%.

2
Tax-Smart Investing: Life in Three Very Separate Baskets

Before the Tax Reform Act of 1986, there were two transcendent principles for tax-smart investing, for investing with the tax consequences of your strategies always in mind.

First, whenever possible you took advantage of the wondrous tax advantages of long-term capital gains.

And second, whenever possible, you sheltered income.

Both have been essentially eliminated by the act.

Indeed the whole face and philosophy of tax-smart investing has been reshaped, at least for the present.

That is not to say that the tax consequences of your investment strategies no longer matter. They do. Take a look at the numbers.

For 1987 you might be in the 38.5% bracket, which really translates into 40–45% when you tack on local taxes. To be sure, that's better than paying more than 50%, as it was, but over 40% is still a meaningful amount of your investment income to share with the IRS.

Before the new law John Connell and his colleagues at

Touche Ross tried to get their clients to observe and obey the long-term capital gains rule.

Basically, as noted in the previous chapter, this meant that they had to hold on to a property, whether it was a stock, bond, or piece of land, for more than six months.

If they did that, they received one of the most generous tax benefits in the whole tax code. When they sold the property, 60% of their entire gain was excluded from taxation.

If they were impatient and sold before the more-than-six-month period was up, their gain was all taxed as "ordinary income," or the same way their salary was taxed, and at their highest level. It could make the difference between paying 50% of the gain in taxes and paying only 20%.

It was as if you were being rewarded or punished, and that was something of the reasoning behind the capital gains benefit in the first place. In theory at least, Congress wanted to encourage you to invest in the economy and invest in a way that would give the economy a chance to benefit. Leave your money in the marketplace, in other words, and you shall be rewarded by the tax break.

There were those who sneered at such reasoning. The capital gains benefit, they contended, was merely a way to make rich folk richer. They would invest with or without such an incentive. And now we may get a chance to see if such critics were right.

With the Tax Reform Act, Congress eliminated the long-term capital gains benefits as of December 31, 1986.

The capital gains that you enjoyed in 1987 will be taxed as ordinary income, up to a maximum of 28%.

Starting with 1988, the maximum is your maximum, which could mean at 33%, according to present schedules.

So, in a way, the 1987 returns you file in 1988 might be your last chance to enjoy some tax benefit from long-term capital gains.

You may also be able to make use of capital losses, long-term or short-term.

As before the reform act, you still may deduct your capital losses from your capital gains, and if you then have long-term capital losses remaining, you may deduct them from short-term capital gains, which otherwise would be taxed to you as ordinary income, up to $3000.

Actually, you get a break with the new law. The ceiling of $3000 remains the same, but it used to take $2 of long-term capital losses to match $1 of short-term gain. Or, $6000 of losses to wipe out $3000 of gains. Now you may match on a dollar-for-dollar basis.

And, as before, if you have those excess long-term losses and no short-term gains, or not $3000 worth, you may apply the long-term losses directly against other ordinary income. Which could mean you shelter $3000 of salary.

Patience Was a Golden Virtue

While the rule prevailed, it dictated an investment philosophy: Be sufficiently patient and don't sell before the long-term capital gains period is up. Most recently this meant more than six months, but before June 23, 1984, it was more than a year.

There were exceptions, of course. If you held a hot stock for three months, it had doubled in value, and you had every reason to believe it was about to drop like a rock, you sold. You took your gain and paid the full tax on it, but you were still better off than losing that gain and suffering a loss.

For the impatient, the numbers were clear and cautionary. If you thought you were making, say, 20% on your investments, you weren't. Not if you were in the old 50% bracket. Right off the top, your taxes knocked your gain in half, so you were down to 10%. Then you had to take into account the current rate of inflation on that meager return. With that factored in, you were down to about 5%. And that was before you calculated your local taxes into the equation.

It was usually somewhat sobering for gunslingers who jumped in and out of the market every other day to confront such numbers. It also helped to answer the question many of them harbored: Where did it all go? I thought I was knocking off all these killings.

Indeed, that pretty well described the way Tom Fusco played the market before John Connell penciled out the above equation for him and was able to convince him to become tax aware and tax smart with his investments.

Taking the long-term view affected the kinds of investments he would make in the first place. It meant he would not leap for every hot tip. It meant that instead he would try to pick stocks of companies that had the potential for growth, if possible in industries that also showed signs of expansion. After all, when he went to sell in more than six months, or previously in more than a year, he wanted the reasonable expectation that his stock would be up.

To Shelter Was Divine

Connell also urged him to invest in real estate.

That suited him and his new tax-smart philosophy in a number of ways. Traditionally, it was an investment that required time, time for properties to appreciate. But Fusco now had the time to give it.

Further, real estate produced write-offs for him, completely legitimate paper losses from mortgage interest expense, from real estate taxes, and most especially from depreciation, all of which "sheltered" his income. Those deductions he received each year for six years from that apartment complex outside of Knoxville he invested in were applied against income from other kinds of investments and activities, including his salary, and saved him more than $100,000 in tax dollars (all of which is discussed in the next chapter).

And that is the second cardinal principle shattered by the reform act, to shelter income whenever possible.

While real estate investments still yield those attractive deductions, the way you may use them and how you may apply them has been totally altered by the creation of "passive" income and losses and the establishment of three different and separate kinds of income.

Three baskets of Income and Losses

The simplest way of grasping this change is to think in terms of three "baskets" of income and losses.

The first is wages, salary or income from a trade or business in which you are actively engaged, and might be called the *active income and loss basket*. The new law uses the term *materially participating* to define this category somewhat.

The second is *portfolio income,* which includes interest, dividends, annuities, royalties not derived from your ordinary trade or business (e.g., an investment in stocks or bonds), plus the gain or loss you realize from the sale of a property that produces such income that was held for investment purposes.

And third, there is the new creature, *passive income and loss.* This encompasses any activity in which you, the taxpayer, do not "materially participate," a phrase that is critical but is not fully defined in the new law.

The new law does say that to qualify you must be "involved in the operations of the activity on a basis which is (A) regular, (B) continuous, and (C) substantial."

That leaves a lot open to question and interpretation. For example, many people do free-lance work in addition to their regular and continuous full-time job. Or, they carry more than one job. In order to "materially participate" must you work at the activity on a full-time basis? May you "materially participate" in more than one activity? The answers, as we'll see, are terribly important. They determine whether you must treat the income from those secondary jobs as passive or active.

Well, according to a subsequent report issued by the Joint Committee on Taxation in an effort to clarify this and countless other aspects of the new law, apparently full-time is not required, but full-time helps.

Not ambiguous are the particular activities Congress carefully included in the passive activity basket.

They start with limited partnerships. Significantly and not by accident, the great majority of tax shelters were structured as limited partnerships.

Also cited for special inclusion as passive activities are nearly all real estate rental activities, as noted another widely used form of investment that offered glittering tax shelter benefits.

One exception to the passive activity basket is any working interest in an oil and gas property, if your liability in the project is not limited (in other words, so long as you are not a limited partner). So, even though you are not materially participating out there in the hot and grimy oil fields, or even materially participating in managing the oil company in an air-conditioned Houston office, *your investment is not passive, and any losses from it may be applied against nonpassive income.*

And that is a key to the changes rendered by the Tax Reform Act of 1986.

Tax-Smart Investing: Life in Three Very Separate Baskets   41

The new law not only creates these three categories of income and losses, these three baskets; it further states that generally you may not mix and match these categories.

And that means a whole new game, a whole new philosophy for investments.

No More Mix and Match

As we saw in the previous chapter, John Connell's client Tom Fusco, the cable TV executive, was able to cut his taxes quite legitimately by tens of thousands of dollars a year because he could take those paper losses—e.g., depreciation he received from his limited partnership investment in the apartment complex—and apply them against the big salary his company paid him.

Today that is pretty much forbidden. Any loss Fusco received from an investment made after August 16, 1986, in a passive activity—and that is what his limited partnership now is—generally could be applied *only* against income from that or other passive activities.

Congress showed something of a heart with this radical change. It allowed a phasing out period of four years. Fusco does not have to go cold turkey. On his investments that were made before August 16, 1986, that produce what are now called *passive losses*, he may treat a portion of them as he did in the old days and apply them against any kind of income.

For 1987 he is allowed deductions on 65% of them; in 1988, on 40%; in 1989, on 20%; in 1990, on 10%; and beginning with 1991, nothing.

So much for tax shelters, which was indeed one of Congress's primary objectives in formulating the "passive" category. It is worth noting, however, that you will be just as much affected by the change in the law whether you made your investment for the primary reason of sheltering income or not. If your investment qualifies as "passive," even though you invested for the good old-fashioned patriotic reason of making a profit on it, but the business turned sour, your losses will be just as "passive" and their use to you just as proscribed as those from Tom Fusco's wily limited partnership.

Starting with your return for 1987, if you have such passive investments, you and your accountant must first figure out the net gain or loss for the category, calculating all of your expenses and deductions from all of your passive activities against all of your income from them. If your losses are greater than your income, you show a loss, a passive loss. Since you may no longer apply such a loss against income from another category, you get no deduction for it in that year (except for the phase-in described above).

It is not wasted, however, since the new law allows you to carry the loss forward to future years without limit, applying it against passive income from those future years.

Finally, when you sell your passive activity investment, you may apply those passive losses you have been carrying forward against your gain on that sale or, if they exceed the gain, against any other passive income you have for that year. And, if they exceed that, against any other income including your otherwise untouchable salary and investment income, without limitation.

There is a happy exception with rental real estate property where you might be allowed a deduction of up to $25,000 in passive losses, if your joint adjusted gross income is below $100,000. Or a portion of that deduction if your AGI is between $100,000 and $150,000. And that special $25,000 deduction may be applied against that nonpassive untouchable income as well. It might, in other words, provide an old-fashioned shelter for your income. (More on this in the next chapter, on real estate investing.)

New Investment Goals

As Fusco said, they have changed all the rules.

As Connell explained to Fusco and his other clients, as a result, they now had to change their investment goals.

While taxes still mattered, they mattered much less when it came to investment decisions. For the most part, that meant defining goals and looking for the investment vehicles to achieve them, unburdened by the usual tax considerations.

If you wanted to put a sunny face on all this, you could say that the changes would make investing somewhat simpler.

Central to the revision, the new law would not permit you to walk away from investments with nearly so much tax-free or tax-deferred income.

However, the tax rates were indeed lower, so some of the blow was softened. In fact, the lowered rates made it relatively easy for Congress to eliminate the capital gains tax benefits. Life, after all, is trade-offs.

One of the objectives Congress had in mind with the Tax Reform Act was to stop people from investing simply in the name of write-offs and deductions.

And to a large degree, they had succeeded.

Today an investor has to look at his real economic return. If he invests $5000, what will his return be before any tax consequences of the investment are considered?

Gone are the days when he could profit from an investment in a losing project. Gone are the days when he could take the losses and deductions from that project and apply them against other income from other sources and end up way ahead.

If he was in the 50% bracket, and a limited partnership in

some mining venture produced $50,000 in losses and deductions for him, that was worth $25,000 to him. Once he applied that $50,000 against other income, there was $25,000 more going into his pocket rather than to the IRS.

The mine was badly operated? The geological surveys gave it almost no chance of producing coal? What did that matter to countless investors? So long as they could mine golden tax losses, who cared about coal? (Of course, there was a day of reckoning for them because there were limits on the number of years the law would permit that mine to report such losses. And after that, the mine produced "phantom income." The investor then had income reported to him by that same rotten mine, even though in fact he never received a dollar, and he had to pay income taxes on that so-called income.)

But to most investors that was so far down the road, so many years in the future, that they couldn't see or imagine it, and they certainly were not going to worry about it. They were simply going to enjoy their losses while they could.

Today, if you invest in a mine, you better know something about the company, the people behind it, the general partners in the deal and their track record on similar deals, and the person selling you the investment, and your accountant had better look hard at their offering statement and their annual report.

Tax-Frees

Tax-free investments still do exist, in the form of municipal bonds. Issued by states, cities, counties, and government authorities—e.g., port, bridge, airport authorities—they are free of federal taxes and state as well, if you buy them from your own state. Buy out-of-state bonds, and you face income taxes from your own state or city (assuming they have an income tax).

The difference in yield between tax-free bonds and taxable bonds has not been very great lately, which makes the tax-free munis appealing.

The problem for many people with munis is that they don't understand bonds in general or munis in particular. These bonds are not subject to the same scrutiny by the Securities Exchange Commission or other federal agencies as corporate bonds, and in addition, ratings on the bonds are confusing and often not very accurate. Whether it is Moody's or Standard and Poor's, the rating normally does not measure very accurately a number of intangibles when it comes to municipalities.

The rating services compile and examine vast amounts of research and data, and they certainly know how to crunch numbers. Where they seem shaky, however, is in political and social judgments. If you have a community in conflict, where perhaps the political leadership is causing business to leave, you have conditions that must be factored into the financial stability of that community. Frequently, ratings are issued on bonds without keen political judgments, and then later, when the turmoil is public and costly, the ratings are lowered. That doesn't help the original buyers.

Tax-free bond funds and trusts can help to cut the risk. They are like mutual funds, a mix of several different kinds of tax-free bonds, preferably from different parts of the country. You invest in the entire fund or trust and its mix.

Investment Interest Deduction

Financing investments under the new law requires attention. As Connell explained to Fusco in the previous chapter, there are new rules on the deductibility of interest you incur for investment funds.

You used to be able to deduct interest on such loans up to your net investment income plus $10,000. That was a potentially large deduction.

The new law says now you may deduct only up to the amount of your net investment income.

One exception is if the financing comes through your principal residence and/or second home.

As noted, so long as you keep the refinancing to the amount you paid for the house plus improvements, you may use the money for almost any purpose you desire, and the entire interest expense you incur on the loan is deductible.

If you decide to finance some investments this way, what kind of return should you realize? After all, you have the interest expense to cover.

Connell's rule of thumb is at least two times the after-tax rate of your interest cost.

So, let's say you take an additional mortgage on your home for $100,000, the bank charges you 10% interest, and you are in the 33% bracket for 1988.

Your after-tax cost is going to be about 6.7% (10% interest rate less 33% tax rate). That means, according to Connell's law, you should make at least some 14% on an after-tax basis with your investment from the mortgage money.

Of course, your return should always be relative to your risk. So, if instead of putting your money into a mixture of strong stocks you go for little-known penny stocks and new issues from Australia, your after-tax rate of return should be more like three or four times your after-tax interest cost.

The emphasis changes today.

While Connell does not recommend specific stocks or other investments, he does review portfolios. Now he looks at them with an eye toward cutting back somewhat on real estate investments because the tax benefits were reduced and because the passive activity laws so restricted what his clients could do with their real estate deductions.

Instead, he suggested to clients that they might look for more stocks with good growth potential, a certain amount of munis, fixed-income investments.

The balance of a portfolio for someone like Fusco would shift from perhaps 70% real estate investments and 30% stocks to more like 50% real estate, 30% stocks, 20% munis and fixed-income investments. He could afford to carry munis and fixed-income investments now that his tax rates would be lower and he could retain so much more of their dividend and interest payments.

Even with the new emphasis, Fusco's portfolio would still be left with quite a bit of real estate, and for good reasons, as we'll see in the next chapter. There are some bright sides of life that not even the new tax law can completely darken.

To deal with Fusco's passive losses, some of which were carried over from past investments and exceeded the 65% allowed in 1987, and some of which would result from new investments, Connell suggested they look at master limited partnerships (MLPs).

These are relatively new real estate vehicles in which you invest in a company that makes real estate investments. As a limited partner your liability is limited, and according to the new law, you receive passive income or losses. In Fusco's case, the goal would be to take passive income and apply his existing passive losses against it to avoid taxes on the income.

Master limited partnerships are special in that they operate like corporations but are structured like partnerships. If they were corporations, there would be double taxation:

the companies would pay corporate taxes, and subsequently you would also pay taxes on whatever you received from the corporation.

But as a partnership an MLP does not pay corporate taxes. It passes income or losses through directly to you and the other limited partners.

They are also special because they are listed on major stock exchanges, making them liquid, which traditional real estate investment vehicles are not.

There is a large question in the eyes of the Treasury Department and congressional tax writers about the purity of MLPs. If they look like corporations and smell like corporations, why don't we call them corporations and tax them accordingly? And indeed Congress might.

Meanwhile, Connell finds them useful for clients like Fusco who have passive losses they want to make current use of.

For another client in the same passive loss predicament, Connell had another strategy. That woman owned a closely held business (see Chapter 5), and the new law allows such a corporation to offset active income from the company's regular business with passive losses. Connell and the woman made a tax-free transfer of her passive loss investments into the closely held corporation, where those losses spared the company tens of thousands of dollars in taxes.

To be sure, with the transfer those investments no longer belonged directly to the woman. They were part of the assets of her corporation. If they produced handsome earnings, those earnings belonged to the corporation, not to the woman. If she wanted to get her hands on those earnings, she would be taxed doubly. That is, first her corporation would have to pay a corporate tax, and then she would pay a tax on what she received.

If the corporation were to hit hard times, those investments might be lost to creditors.

Nevertheless, for present tax-planning purposes, the woman was much better off with the transfer. And, as we'll see in Chapters 4 and 5 in the discussion of small businesses, creating wealth within a closely held business can offer a number of advantages.

Connell developed a different plan for a client who was near retirement. The man was a great believer in tax shelters in the old days, and now he worried as he approached age 73 that he was never going to be able to "sop up," as he put it, all the passive losses in his portfolio. (They would be "sopped up" on his final return, if they still remained.)

He was an independent insurance broker, quite successful, and some eight years before had brought his daughter into the business. He had decided that she was ready to take over the business with him assisting as a consultant. Many of his own customers were retired or dead, and basically he would continue to service them but steer new business to his daughter. She had developed a considerable business of her own.

For tax purposes the insurance agency operated as a sole proprietorship, and every year the man accounted for his income and expenses from the business on a Schedule C.

Connell's plan was to change it to a limited partnership. The man would retire, not be a consultant, and become a limited partner in it, and so according to the new law all of his income from it would be passive. That was what he wanted, in order to "sop up" the substantial passive losses he had.

His daughter would become the general partner in the company, and since she "materially participated" in it, her income from it would qualify as active, which was what she wanted.

Checklist: Chapter 2

Tax-smart strategies and perspectives for you to discuss with your tax professional:

1. Before the Tax Reform Act of 1986, there were two transcendent principles for tax-smart investing.

First, whenever possible, you took advantage of the tax benefits of long-term capital gains in which 60% of your gain was excluded from taxes.

Second, whenever possible, you invested with a view to sheltering income.

Both have been essentially eliminated by the act.

2. Taxes still matter. For 1987, if you are in the 38.5% bracket, you could be sharing 40-45% of your investment income with the IRS when local taxes are added on.

However, if you have long-term capital gains to report for 1987, they will be taxed as ordinary income, which is to say at the same rate as your salary—but not higher than 28%. After 1987, they will be taxed at your rate, which could be 33%.

3. You may still deduct long-term capital losses from short-term capital gains, up to $3000, or from other ordinary income.

4. Investing with long-term capital gains in mind meant investing with a long view. You looked for stocks that had the potential for growth over your holding period. You also looked for real estate. Again, you could give it the time to appreciate, and meanwhile you could enjoy the considerable deductions real estate investment brought you, deductions that could be applied against and "shelter" any other income you had.

5. The new law has eliminated such sheltering by creating three categories of income and losses and essentially not allowing you to mix and match one with the other.

There is a basket that includes wages and salary or income from a trade or business in which you are "materially participating."

There is another for portfolio income, your interest, dividends, gains from the sale of stock, bonds, property in general that you held for investment purposes.

There is a completely new and central category, passive income and loss, which means first of all any activity in which you do not "materially participate."

It specifically includes all limited partnerships, which is the form of most tax shelters.

It also includes nearly all rental real estate activities, which had been another source of tax shelter benefits.

Any working interest in an oil and gas property is not included, so long as you are not a limited partner, even though you are not materially participating.

6. Where you used to be able to apply the losses from activities now called *passive* to any other kind of income, generally you may not any longer. Now any passive losses you have may be applied against passive income only. There is an exception with rental properties, which allows a deduction of up to $25,000 in passive losses against any other kind of income, salary, investment, whatever, if you show a joint adjusted gross income of less than $100,000. Between $100,000 and $150,000 this deduction gets phased out at the rate of 50 cents for every dollar of income.

7. Today investors must look to their real economic return on an investment, the return before any tax consequences are considered. Even where an investment might still produce tax-deductible paper losses, since they may not be applied against nonpassive income, investment objectives must change, which indeed was the intention of Congress in writing this part of the new law.

8. Tax-free investments do exist in the form of municipal bonds, bond funds, and bond trusts.

9. The interest you may deduct on loans for investment purposes is now limited to your net investment income. You may, however, take funds from the refinancing of your principal residence and/or second home—up to the amount you paid for them plus improvements—use the money for investments, and all of the interest on those funds will be deductible.

The after-tax return on investments with such funds should be equal to at least two times your after-tax cost of the mortgage. With high-risk investments, the return should be more like three or four times your after-tax cost.

10. There are strategies available for people who want to make current use of excess passive losses.

For example, investing in master limited partnerships, which are new kinds of real estate investments. As limited partnerships they produce passive income or losses, and an investment in an MLP that produces such income will allow you to take that income, apply your excess passive losses against it, and avoid any taxes on it.

Since MLPs are structured as partnerships, not corporations, they avoid corporate taxes, passing income and losses directly through to the limited partners. They are also sold through major stock exchanges, making them liquid, which traditional real estate investment vehicles were not.

They are, however, under examination by Congress, which might recharacterize them and tax them as corporations.

11. For owners of closely held corporations, there is the possibility of transferring investments with passive losses into the corporation. The new law permits a closely held to offset active income from its regular business with passive losses, which could result in a tax saving for the corporation.

12. A partnership may be split and produce passive in-

come for a limited partner and active income for its "materially participating" general partner.

This strategy might be useful where the partners have different needs, especially where one with excess passive losses is planning to take a less active role in the business.

3
Real Estate:
The Golden Days Turn Silver

It was the great American juggling act. It was fun, and it was profitable. It was even chic.

Here were all these clients of Douglas Banks, one of the national real estate directors of Touche Ross in Washington, and they were having the time of their lives.

They were investing in real estate, and thanks to the U.S. government, it seemed they couldn't lose. In fact, the government was something of a partner in their deals.

The game went like this: You made your investment, and the government in a sense increased it.

It said you could take a variety of deductions related to your real estate project.

There was the interest paid to the bank for the mortgage. There were the local real estate taxes.

There was also an almost magical deduction called *depreciation*. Every year, the government said, assume that the value of your building depreciates, declines in value. Wear and tear. So, it's only fair that you may deduct a portion of the cost of the building each year. There were formulas and depreciation tables, and at one point you could choose between what was called *accelerated depreciation* and *straight-line depreciation*.

As the name suggests, accelerated depreciation allowed you to take higher amounts in the earlier years, less in the later years of the life of the property. Straight-line was a set, unvaried figure, year after year. The life of the property depended on the kind of property, but at one time you might have invested in a rental property assigned a 15-year life.

What this meant was that every year for 15 years you were entitled to a depreciation deduction that would have been the cost of the building divided by 15, if it were straight-line, or the adjusted amount for accelerated.

Now—and here's where the magic comes in—all of these deductions were permitted, even if the actual value of your property was going up, not down.

When you sold the property, there was a bit of a reckoning in that the amount you had deducted over the years for depreciation was figured as part of your gain in the sale. And, of course, you had to pay a tax on your gain.

So in a way the tax benefit of the depreciation deduction was a loan from the U.S. government. You eventually had to pay the government back, but until then you had the use of its money, interest-free.

And, in fact, you didn't even have to pay it all back. When you sold the property, if you had owned it for more than a year, a holding period that was subsequently lowered to only six months and a day, you could have a long-term capital gain for a portion of it, and the tax on that was a maximum of only 20%.

Depending on the kind of investment, this meant that you might receive deductions, paper losses, of two or three times what you invested.

Invest $25,000 in a real estate deal, receive deductions worth $50,000 a year. You could take those $50,000 in paper losses and apply them against, say, $50,000 in salary. That meant you didn't have to pay any taxes on the $50,000 of salary.

Over and above this, deals in real estate and other kinds of investments that promised considerably higher deductions, maybe $4 of deductions for every $1 you invested, were available. Many of these were shams where the underlying property or product was worthless and by a combination of tricks the deductions were inflated.

Even with the legitimate shelters there were some limits. Even though the government was your partner, there were limits, for example, on the depreciation, and after a certain number of years you could run out of depreciation, and the property could produce what was called *phantom income.* Like the losses, phantom income was income on paper only. As noted in Chapter 2, your shelter limited partnership, for example, never sent you a dollar, yet you were still taxed on that income, just as if you had received it in crisp new dollar bills.

And, as noted, you had to account for depreciation when you sold the property.

Some of this was played out through large public limited partnership offerings. You along with thousands of others invested in apartment complexes and shopping centers.

But for many of Banks's clients, the game was often played much closer to home in a much more personal way. They invested in single-family dwellings. Less exotic than the high-rise development in Houston, perhaps, but it could be just as profitable.

To begin with, they knew the joys of leverage.

No other investment matches real estate when it comes to leverage, which allows you to buy a property by putting down only a small percentage of its value.

This benefit has nothing to do with tax advantages. But it

means that the rate of return on your investment can be increased substantially.

If you buy a single-family residence with a view toward renting it out, and the place costs $100,000, you may have to invest only 20% of that. You put up $20,000 of your money, not $100,000 of your money. (You borrow the $80,000 difference from the bank and receive a nice tax deduction on the interest you pay it.)

If the real value of the property appreciates at only 5% a year, that translates into a 25% return to you on your investment.

Furthermore, this kind of real estate investing is fairly simple. The average person can grasp it and manage it. But investing the same money in the stock market could be considerably more complicated and require a good deal more sophistication and effort to control.

It was the best of times.

New Law, New Problems

Mary Berger wanted to turn back the clock. She had been one of Banks's clients for years, going back to the days when she worked for the civil rights section of the Justice Department and made her first real estate investment. Now, as a lawyer in private practice, she was in Banks's office throwing up her hands.

She had decided that the whole Tax Reform Act of 1986 was a plot to get her, probably manipulated by her politically well-connected ex-husband. Not only was her rental property about to go sour, or so she thought, but she also appeared to be headed for trouble with her vacation home, which she rented out part of the year.

When she bought the rental property for $100,000 and balanced off the operating expenses on it, including her 30-

year mortgage against her rental income, she was in the hole around $300 a month.

But her huge silent partner, the U.S. government, came to the rescue. She took accelerated depreciation over a mere 19-year life, and that gave her a deduction of about $6000 a year in the early years.

Her ex-husband's earnings at that time pushed them into the 50% bracket, which meant that the $6000 depreciation deduction was worth $3000 a year that Mary could hang on to. And that $3000 pretty well wiped out her annual deficit on the project.

Beyond that, according to her plan when she bought it, she would sell the place after some five years, assuming the market went up, as it did, and enjoy the low 20% capital gains tax then in effect.

Over five years, according to that plan, with $6000 in depreciation a year, she would have $30,000 in that deduction alone, worth about $15,000 in taxes saved. When she sold the place, she'd have to pay back only $6000 of those savings ($30,000 depreciation deduction times 20% capital gains tax equals $6000).

Now she wasn't quite sure what would happen. She was thinking of selling the place, she told Banks, even without the benefit of capital gains rates. But she wanted to find out what the results would be if she did that. Or, what the new picture would look like if she held on to the property. And she also wanted to know what she might be entitled to under the new law, if she sold it and bought a new place.

Banks led her through the dark scenario.

Since she had owned the property long before the new law went into effect, she would still be entitled to her old benefits, if she kept the property. However, with tax rates reduced significantly, the tax benefits of her deductions would drop proportionately. She was now in a 28% bracket, with local taxes pushing it to 35%. What that means is that on the $6000 loss, Banks explained, instead of the government's lending you $3000, the amount drops to $2100.

On a new property, she wouldn't have even $6000 in losses today because the depreciation rates had been completely overhauled. For a residential rental property, they've practically been cut in half. Before, you could depreciate on an accelerated basis over 19 years. Now, there is no accelerated basis, only straight-line, and the life of your property has gone up to 27½ years.

The depreciation deduction is going to be cut to $3000. And if Mary would end up with only 35% of that, she'd receive only $1050 in reduced taxes, rather than the old $3000.

She was aghast. Her situation looked like an unmitigated disaster. If she kept the current property, she'd be losing at least $1500 a year ($3600 a year out of pocket cash expenses less $2100 tax savings). And a new property would cost her more, about $2500 a year.

Banks told her that unfortunately her arithmetic was pretty good.

However, she thought she glimpsed a salvation. Suppose she applied those losses against what she described as her obscenely high income. She was now earning $175,000 to $200,000 a year as a partner in her Washington law firm.

A nice strategy, Banks told her, but it wouldn't work anymore. He explained the new passive activity rules to her and the restrictions on mixing and matching passive losses against active income. Like many of his clients, Mary had heard about these new rules, read a bit on them, but never realized how they would land on her.

Active Yet Still Passive

To begin with, all real estate rental investments were cited specifically by the Tax Reform Act as "passive," Banks explained.

Mary immediately objected. She herself ran her property. She had a super who maintained the place, but there wasn't a decision that didn't come from her. How could anyone say she was passive in the investment? She was most definitely active.

To a degree, the government did recognize that, Banks told her. In the new law it's called *active participation*. But if she could believe it, that is different from *materially participating*, which in most cases determines whether the income or losses are active or passive.

Still, if you are an active participant, they give you a break, he explained. The law says that any losses you have from the rental property may be applied against income from other passive investments. They don't necessarily have to be real estate, but they have to be passive. So, generally speaking, she wouldn't be able to apply the losses against earnings from her law practice.

He went on to say that there was an exception for active participants, which caused her to sit up very straight. Once more, however, he had bad news. The exception probably would not apply to her. She earned too much money.

If your passive rental activity produces up to $25,000 in excess losses, i.e., deductions and expenses more than income, you may apply those losses against any other income, just like a shelter in the old days.

But the $25,000 was phased out between $100,000 and $150,000 of adjusted gross income. For every dollar she showed over $100,000, she lost the current use of $.50 of

Real Estate: The Golden Days Turn Silver 61

the loss. If her AGI were $110,000, she would be $10,000 over and lose $5000 of the losses. At $150,000, all $25,000 is wiped out, which unfortunately was where Mary would find herself.

So, she might end up with a few dollars to deduct, but probably not much.

However, the law will allow her to carry the unused losses forward, and if she has a year where she comes up with passive income, she can apply them against that. Or, in the year that she sells the property, she may apply them against any gain she realizes on the sale of the property and, if they exceed that, against other income.

Also the law would permit a phase-in break on losses from investments made before August 16, 1986: For 1987, 65% of losses could be applied against any income, passive or otherwise, with the remaining 35% treated as passive only, and applied against passive income only, or carried forward; for 1988, only 40% could be applied against any income; for 1989, only 20%; for 1990, 10%; and after that, it is all passive.

Beware the AMT

But just so you don't think you're getting too much of a break, Banks went on, when and if you do apply your passive losses, you now have to account for them in the new alternative minimum tax computation (see Chapter 1).

He reviewed the AMT with its system of adding back preference items and adjustment items. It was always a worrisome thing for his clients who were heavy real estate investors, because so many of the preference items were tax benefits from real estate.

The danger for Mary if she qualified for the AMT was that it would affect her benefits from any real estate deal. If she looked at a deal with deductions, even if they were less than before, she figured that in her 28% bracket these deductions would still save her 28 cents on every dollar.

But if she fell into the AMT, she would have to pay the 21% AMT tax on everything, including those deductions. So, in effect, she would reduce her tax by only 7%, not 28%.

But as Banks recalled Mary's situation, the AMT was at least one problem she wouldn't have to worry about.

Mary was silent for a while. What he was painting was much bleaker than she had ever expected. Still, so far as her property was concerned, she thought she had no choice but to sell it, even without a capital gains benefit. She thought she could get $150,000 for it. How much of that would she have to pay in taxes?

Banks scratched out a few numbers on a small pad by his phone. He started with her $50,000 gain, to which he would have to add her depreciation as further gain. He said he would have to double-check her file, but roughly he thought she had taken about $26,000 in depreciation. So, say for now, that would mean taxes on $76,000.

In her 28% percent bracket, figuring 35% with local taxes, she would owe about $26,000, less 35 cents on every dollar of passive losses she'd accumulated.

The Beauty of a Swap

Mary was desperate. Was there no way for her to avoid such a beating? she asked Banks.

Banks had one strategy to propose. It was called a *swap*.

A swap is basically a trade of real estate properties in which both parties have the same amount of equity. And most importantly in Mary's case, it is a way of deferring,

Real Estate: The Golden Days Turn Silver

possibly avoiding, the income taxes she faced on a sale of the property.

She now held a property worth $150,000, but she still carried a mortgage of about $80,000. So her equity in the property was $70,000 ($150,000 less $80,000).

She had to find two things: a buyer for her property and another property that was worth buying for $350,000.

Then she would in effect tell her buyer to go buy the $350,000 property. Assume he would have to put down 20%, or $70,000, for that.

He'd bring the other property to her, and she would swap her property—in which she also has $70,000 of equity. They would both have the same amount of money invested, and he would end up owning her property while she would own the other more expensive place. (In practice, the other buyer could refinance her property so that he would end up with much less than $70,000 of his own money involved. Rather, more like 20% of its value or $30,000.)

And she would not have to pay any tax on the $76,000 gain she received. The law would allow her to defer recognition of that gain.

She would have to diminish the depreciable portion of the new property by her $76,000, which would give her that much less of a depreciation deduction each year. But these days depreciation wasn't worth that much anyway, with the new tables and a 27½-year life for the building.

Too Good to Be True?

Mary thought the swap sounded wonderful. She wondered only when she was going to get hit. Somewhere she was going to have to pay taxes, she was sure. Otherwise it was all too wonderful to be legal.

Banks assured her that it was legal, but if she sold the $350,000 property, then she'd have capital gains taxes. However, he quickly added, there was no law that required her to sell it.

What else would she do with it? she wondered. Just hold on to it?

Or make another swap, Banks told her. He had a number of clients who started with one single-family house, fixed and improved it, and then swapped. They took the new property and did it all over again, maybe four, five times over a period of years, and never had to pay any income taxes at all during that time on those trades. Yet they kept multiplying the value of their real estate.

Could she do that? Mary wanted to know. Continually avoid taxes, indefinitely?

Not avoid, Banks corrected her, merely defer. If you finally sell, you pay the taxes. But, there is also no law that says you must ever sell.

In other words, she might go on swapping for many years. She never sells, so she never pays taxes on the gains. And then finally she dies. At that point, the property goes into her estate, and she gets what's called a *stepped-up value*. All of the gains will disappear so far as income taxes are concerned. If her $70,000 investment has by that time ballooned to $500,000, she is spared the income taxes on the entire $500,000.

Mary declared it the best thing she had ever heard.

Not surprisingly, there was a trade-off. That $500,000 would then be part of her estate, and the estate could face estate taxes on it, Banks warned her.

Mary laughed. "You think I'm going to worry about that? When I'm dead and gone? Compared with no taxes for the rest of my lifetime?" She shook her head. "Now solve the rest of my real estate problems."

The Personal/Rental Monster

She had something of a laundry list, and next on it was her second home.

Normally, she had used the farm in Virginia as a weekend retreat during the summer. Since it was near a college, she was able to rent it out the rest of the year.

At Banks's direction, she kept a careful record of how much time went to rental as opposed to personal use, and all of the deductible expenses connected with the house were divided accordingly. One way or another, in the end she made use of all the deductions.

But now she had heard that in some horrible way the passive activity rules were going to limit her use of those proportioned deductions.

Protecting Deductions

This one has been a terrible mess, Banks told her. When the law first was passed, nothing was clear. There were about 13 possible scenarios. It was months before it got somewhat clarified, though it's still quite complicated.

As before, he told her, you start out by keeping track of all expenses and dividing them between rental and personal use.

Then you have to figure out the number of days for personal use. If it amounts to fewer than 15 days a year, or less than 10% of the time you rent the place out in a year, you are allowed to claim rental expenses including depreciation in excess of rental income as a passive loss. The personal portion of the interest expense is also treated as a passive loss.

However, if you use the place for personal use for 15 days or more (unless that is less than 10% of the days you rent the property), then you may not claim expenses in excess of rental income and so have no passive loss. But all of the mortgage interest may be taken as a personal deduction.

Expenses incurred in connection with the renting of the house—items like the rental portion of the utilities, the heating oil, the caretaker, general maintenance of the place —will be subject to a ceiling. They may be deducted only up to the amount of rental income the property produces. Whatever amount exceeds that is lost. No deduction, nothing carried forward, all gone.

Avoiding the Passive Category

Then there was the whole question of how the passive activity rules come into play.

For example, if Mary used the house personally for less than 15 days a year and rented it out for more than 15 days a year, then all the deductions including the mortgage interest would be attributable to the passive rental activity. She would not be able to take any of them as a personal deduction.

And given the amount of the interest deduction plus the depreciation deduction, most likely she would end up with a passive loss.

She had one other passive activity, the single-family dwelling she rented out. But it did not produce any passive income that she could apply against the passive losses from the second-home rental. That meant she would have a passive loss to carry forward.

Whether or not that was good news depended on her adjusted gross income and whether she would be eligible for any of the special deduction of up to $25,000 in excess losses they had reviewed earlier.

For some people, with AGIs below $100,000 or between $100,000 and $150,000, that $25,000 could represent a tax shelter, if their AGI qualified. As they had already decided, it was unlikely that Mary would qualify for much if any of that deduction.

So the decision on the best way to juggle a second home between personal use and rental for Mary or anyone depended to some extent on income level.

In Mary's case, using the house herself for three months and renting it out the remaining nine months each year, she would be able to take the entire mortgage expense as a personal deduction, as noted.

As for the rest of the expenses and deductions in the equation, Banks told her they'd have to do some arithmetic. Certainly the rental income is helpful in paying for the house. But maybe she'd be better off doing what other high-income clients of his were doing, forgetting about rentals for now. They are using the vacation homes themselves, period. All depends on the numbers.

Raw Land

Mary was beginning to wonder about the wisdom of real estate as an investment at all these days.

That was up to her, Banks told her. But she should not lose sight of the fact that, new law or not, real estate was still a limited commodity. You still can invest in it on a leveraged basis. However, now your objectives have to be different. No more rubbing your hands together and saying, What are the losses? Give me more losses. Now you have to invest in a kind of old-fashioned way, for economic gain. How good is this property? What are its real chances of appreciation? Where can I make money on my investment? Now you have to approach it that way, keeping one eye on the passive-active consequences.

Mary said she was thinking about raw land.

Banks didn't want to discourage her further, but raw land could be tricky. He had clients who had made fortunes by investing in raw land, others who had suffered badly.

One of the problems with it is that it usually doesn't produce any income; it just sits there. That can make the cost of carrying it expensive. To lessen the load one client with land in New Mexico is trying to farm jojoba beans until the day when Santa Fe finally spreads out to his land.

But the wait can be unpredictably long. And a lot can happen while you're waiting. Other clients bought land along a highway in Ohio. Perfect for industrial development, they thought. But interest rates went up, and no one was building. Then they got hit with zoning restrictions. They must have held and paid for the property for 10 years before they finally unloaded it, with hardly any appreciation.

Taxes don't give you much relief with raw land either. You may not depreciate land under any circumstances. If you have a building on a piece of land, the depreciation is based completely on the building. Nothing is allowed for the land. So there is zero depreciation with raw land.

Usually the only deductions you have are for real estate taxes and mortgage interest, and even there you could have a problem.

The tax law views raw land as an investment, while most people view it as real estate.

That means that it is subject to the new investment income or portfolio rules. The big change here, as noted, is in the amount of interest deduction you are now allowed. Under the old law, you could deduct up to the amount of your net investment income, plus $10,000. Now the limit is your net investment income.

Mary reminded him that she did not have a whole lot of investment income.

In that case, she had to be careful. She might not be able

to deduct the whole mortgage interest expense, have to carry it forward into other years. That could make the investment much less interesting.

"God, don't you have any good news?"

"The good news with raw land is that you can make big money if you know what you're doing or you're lucky—preferably both."

He told her about one client who along with four friends bought land a number of years ago outside Washington. A huge shopping center was built on it. The client's investment was $10,000. He recently sold out for $15 million.

Mary smiled. She liked that kind of story.

Another client, he told her, not long ago had an option on a major piece of land in Maryland, but he didn't have the cash to do the deal. Instead he found a Japanese firm that was willing to buy out his contract. The man made $1 million on the transaction and never even took title to the land. Location, timing, luck.

That was exactly the kind of thing she had in mind.

"I wish you well," he replied. "But if you go into raw land, do it with someone who knows what they're doing. It'll help."

She gave him a sharp look and promised to do just that.

Historic Buildings

Mary reached into her briefcase and fished out a folder. She had been approached about a historic building. Did that make any sense? The guy who was pushing it claimed it was one of the last shelters left, with big credits, which he maintained were even better than deductions.

With a historic building, he told her, you get all the tax write-offs, you make money on your investment, and you help a good cause, restoring a fine old building. Was there any truth to all that?

There was some, Banks told her.

The developer is telling her the truth when he says that a credit is better than a deduction. A deduction is taken off your earned income, cutting the amount of income on which your tax is finally based. If Mary is in the 28% bracket, a deduction saves her 28 cents on the dollar. But a credit is taken dollar for dollar against the total income tax she would otherwise owe.

By and large investment credits were eliminated by the new law. And while it looked for a while that Congress would also wipe out the credits allowed for rehabilitations, in the end it decided to leave them but cut them back.

You can still get a credit of 20% of the restoration costs if the building is certified as a historic building, 10% of those costs if it is a nonhistoric building that was placed in service before 1936.

There's a maximum of $7000 in such credits you may take in a year, that $7000 being the equivalent of a $25,000 loss. As with the $25,000 passive loss exception, this credit also phases out. In this case, you lose it if your adjusted gross income goes between $200,000 and $250,000.

You need a pretty large deal to invest in. A small project, say two or three partners, could well throw off more credits than they could use.

There are stiff requirements for structures that qualify for the credits, and getting a building certified by the Department of Interior can be long and costly.

Still, Banks felt, given the right deal, Mary might be able to eliminate up to $7000 of income taxes and have the chance of a fair return on her investment.

He asked her if she had a prospectus on a specific project for him to review.

She did not, but she would get one, since it seemed like something they should definitely put on the "possible" list.

PIGs and PALs

Mary went back to her folder, sifting through papers and notes. Without looking up, she muttered that she wasn't sure where she was going to get the cash to invest in any of these things anyway. Especially if she did the swap instead of selling the rental property and reinvesting that money.

That was simple, Banks told her. She should refinance her home.

She had heard about lots of people doing that.

It could be a big advantage these days, he told her. All of the interest on her new mortgage would be completely deductible to her, as always. She wouldn't have to worry about the new rules on rental property, or passive losses, investment income deductions, or anything. She would be entitled to the full deduction, assuming she followed the new refinancing limits, which he explained. (See Chapter 1.)

She wanted his opinion on another project. The guy peddling this one actually called it a new kind of real estate investment. Limited partnership, like the old days, but instead of losses, like the old days, this one produces income.

Banks could hardly see anything wrong with an investment that produced income. Question was, how much?

Not that much. The promoter compared it to a municipal bond. Not a great rate of return, but most of it, he said, would be tax-free. The best part of all is that the income would be passive income, so she could take any passive losses she had and apply them against these gains, and in that sense it would almost be like the good old days.

Banks was familiar with these new creatures, affectionately known as *PIGs, passive income generators,* and they were interesting. Basically they were one of the ways the market was trying to respond to the needs of old real estate investors who suddenly find themselves with passive losses they don't know what to do with. In other words, these deals are meant to generate, as the promoter said, passive gains. (Their counterpart, *PALs,* produce passive activity losses.)

Some of the income will be sheltered, since a certain amount of deductions will still be allowed—depreciation on a limited scale—but they are really not in that sense like municipal bonds. The income from munis is tax-free; the income from these deals is tax-deferred. Like the old days, when the partnership sells the property, there is an adjustment for the depreciation taken over the years.

Why Sacrifice Leverage?

The biggest difference with these investments, however, was in the approach to leveraging themselves. Unlike the traditional real estate investment, which took fullest advantage of leverage possibilities, these partnerships buy their properties with lots of cash, anywhere from 40% or 50% to 100%.

The advantage from their point of view is that they do not have much or any financing. There is little or no mortgage on the property, so little or no interest expense. That greatly reduces or eliminates that potential deduction, which would create passive problems for the intended investor anyway.

And an unleveraged property, of course, is much more likely to produce income, in this case passive income.

Now, that might serve the needs of certain investors who feel they must have passive income more than anything in life. But it also eliminates the great advantage of any real estate investment—leverage.

If you put down 100% cash, your percent of gain on your

investment is going to be very low. Earlier, he reminded her, they were talking about using an equity of $70,000 to acquire a property worth $350,000. That's the traditional use of leverage, and it is a benefit unique to real estate. These deals throw that away.

Beyond that drawback, such an investment wasn't really appropriate for Mary in Banks's opinion. She didn't have a lot of passive losses to absorb.

Mary agreed, but nevertheless she had found the promoter very convincing. He reminded her of one of those syndicators from the old days promising all those write-offs. "No reason for an intelligent woman like you to pay any taxes at all," they used to say.

That was the problem, Banks told her. So many people got sucked into that no-tax mentality. Half the time they didn't know what they were investing in; all they knew was the thing was going to give them write-offs of three to one, five to one, a hundred to one.

Mary defended herself. She was never that bad.

That was true, Banks admitted. And fortunately not one of his clients ever went too crazy. People who did are jamming the tax court today fighting with the IRS over hundreds of thousands of dollars in disallowed shelter deductions.

Mary asked him if she should infer that his good news for the day was that at least she didn't have to come up with hundreds of thousands of dollars or go to jail.

Life was not that grim, he told her.

Mary wasn't so sure, at least so far as her real estate life was concerned. She had done nicely with real estate investments in the past with his guidance, and she would like to do so in the future. But for the most part he had painted such a dark picture.

Not necessarily so, he protested. There was no pretending that you could enjoy the tax benefits of the good old days. You could not.

But what in the world is wrong with putting down only 20% of the cost of a piece of property and having it appreciate over, say, five years and selling it for three times what you paid for it? With a certain amount of tax benefits along the way? What's so terrible about that?

"Looked at that way," she replied, "I suppose, nothing. Absolutely nothing. Except then I really have to know what I'm doing."

Checklist: Chapter 3

Tax-smart strategies and perspectives for you to consider and discuss with your tax professional:

1. Before the Tax Reform Act of 1986 you were entitled to a fairly generous depreciation deduction on a rental property, a deduction that could be applied against other income. That amount of tax saving generally enabled you to carry a property, even if its earnings did not meet its expenses.

When you sold the property, the depreciation you had taken over the years had to be figured as part of your taxable gain on the sale.

But if you owned the property for more than a year, a holding period that was subsequently cut to more than six months, then a portion of your gain on it qualified as a long-term capital gain. Sixty percent of that gain was excluded from taxes, so if you were in the then highest bracket of 50%, your maximum tax on the gain could be only 20%, or 50% of the remaining taxable 40%.

Since the Tax Reform Act, depreciation still exists but on a diminished scale.

With any new purchases, the amount you are allowed to deduct each year has been cut.

Further, with a drop in the rates for individuals, the deduction means correspondingly less in dollars. A $6000 deduction in a year meant a tax savings of at least $3000 in your 50% federal bracket, with local taxes being factored in on top of that and adding to your tax savings. But if you are currently in a 28% federal bracket, and local taxes bring you to 35%, the saving will be more like $2100.

Furthermore, long-term capital gains advantages have been eliminated. The tax on your gain will be the same as the tax on any other income you have, a maximum of 28–33%, or considerably above the old 20% ceiling.

2. In addition, the new law applies passive activity rules to your real estate rental investment, which generally place all such investments in the passive category. Any losses from such an investment may be applied only against passive income, not against other kinds, e.g., salary from your job, as was permitted before tax reform.

One exception to this will allow you to apply up to $25,000 of such passive losses against any other income, if you are an "active participant" in the real estate rental project and your adjusted gross income is below $100,000. Over $100,000, and you lose fifty cents of the loss for every dollar of income. At $110,000, you are $10,000 over, so you lose $5000 of the loss. At $150,000, you have wiped out the whole loss.

Though you might not be able to apply such passive losses in the same year they are realized, you may carry them forward and apply them against your gain when the property is sold. If they exceed the amount of your gain, you may apply them against any other income.

If you have passive losses from investments made before the law became effective, August 16, 1986, you are allowed to phase out your current application of those losses, applying them against nonpassive income as before, on this schedule:

In 1987 you could apply 65% of your losses against any income, passive or otherwise, with the 35% remaining to be treated as passive only and applied against passive income only or carried forward; in 1988, only 40%; in 1989, 20%; in 1990, 10%; and after that, it is all passive under the new definitions and rules.

3. Leverage is an investment practice that allows you to buy a property using only a small percentage of the cost with your own capital while borrowing the balance. Typically on commercial properties you put down 20% of the cost and borrow the balance. This enables you to buy considerably more with your money than if you were required to pay 100% for a property out of your own assets.

While leverage is an investment principle that is separate from taxes, the interest you pay on the borrowed portion of your investment will be deductible against passive income.

4. A swap is an exchange of properties in which you and another party have the same amount of capital invested. From a tax perspective, there is no tax to pay at the time of the exchange. The tax is deferred on the ostensible gain. By swapping you may trade one property for a more valuable one—assuming the amount you have invested in your property is equal to the amount your counterpart has invested in the other—and all the taxes you would otherwise have to pay on the gain may be deferred.

When you finally sell, there will be a tax. However, if you do not sell, but continue swapping and die, the property will pass into your estate, and there will be no income tax on all of the appreciation. As part of your estate, the value of the property could be subject to estate taxes.

5. Under the new law, certain deductions that you previously enjoyed may be limited by the passive activity rules. If you split a vacation home between personal and rental use and use it personally less than 15 days per year or less than 10% of the time you rent it out in a year, it becomes a

rental property subject to the passive rules. Under those circumstances all of the deductions are applied to rental use, including the deduction for mortgage interest, which you would otherwise be able to declare as a personal deduction.

You have to keep track of the amount of time the home is used for personal as opposed to rental, and expenses and deductions may then be proportioned.

If you use the house less than 15 days, many expenses may be deducted from rental income; e.g., the proportionate expenses from utilities, heating, maintenance of the house, and depreciation. If you use it more than 15 days and not less than 10% of the time you rent it out, then the deductions will be limited to the extent of rental income. To the extent that they exceed the income, they are not allowed as deductions and simply dissolve.

Under the complicated formula created by the Tax Reform Act, you may end up with a number of your deductions falling into the passive rental loss category. They are first applied against passive income, and to the extent that they exceed that they might be applied against other income, depending on your income level.

If you use the house personally less than the 15 days, you might be able to use the excess losses as something of a tax shelter. As noted, the new law permits the application of up to $25,000 in real estate losses against any other income—e.g., salary, investment—if your joint adjusted gross income is less than $100,000.

That special deduction phases out as your joint AGI rises between $100,000 and $150,000, when it becomes zero.

If you have excess passive losses, they are not lost. They may be carried forward until you sell the vacation home, at which time they may be applied against your gain on the sale and, if they exceed that, against any other income from any source, even if it is not passive.

Review this with your tax pro. Doing the arithmetic for your own particular case should tell you if you have to restrict your use.

6. Raw land is a risky form of real estate investment. It normally produces no income to help pay carrying costs, and while it's sitting there, external conditions can affect it. Zoning laws, for example, can change its potential value.

Under the TRA, raw land is subject to the new investment income or portfolio rules.

7. While investment credits have largely been eliminated by the new law, credits are still allowed for rehabilitations of historic buildings: 10% of the costs of rehabilitation on a building placed in service before 1936, 20% on a certified historic building. The credit is phased out if your adjusted gross income goes from $200,000 to $250,000.

8. The Tax Reform Act now allows you to refinance your primary residence up to the amount you paid for it plus the cost of improvements, and that money may be invested as you choose.

The interest on your refinanced loan is completely deductible to you. If you use the money to invest in real estate, the interest deduction remains deductible and is not subject to the new passive activity rules.

9. Instead of investing in real estate in the traditional way and taking fullest advantage of leverage possibilities, the new unleveraged real estate deals are for all or nearly all cash. One result is that, instead of creating losses, they create income, passive income. That is their objective, to create passive income that may be applied against passive losses, which many real estate investors now find themselves holding since the tax reform changes. However, for other investors, such a deal is of questionable value, since it does eliminate the great economic advantage of leverage, of putting down only a small percentage of the market value of the property.

10. In recent years, great numbers of real estate investors lost sight of the economic value of their investments and their properties, focused as they were on the potential losses from depreciation and other sources created by the properties. The Tax Reform Act has radically reduced the value of those deductions, which means that now an investor in real estate must invest with the economic opportunities of the investment foremost in mind, rather than with a no-tax mentality.

4
Your Own Corporation:
A Shell Full of Tax Benefits

Phoenix, Arizona, is something of a land of growth and opportunity. From his downtown office, William L. Raby, Senior Tax Partner of Touche Ross, looks out upon miles of valley to the distant mountains, a stretch of land that was desert not 30 years ago.

It is all buildings today—offices, warehouses, stores and shopping malls, shiny suburban communities. Raby has watched his city grow and sprawl, with much of that action passing over his desk. Active in the Phoenix business community for years, head of the Arizona Chamber of Commerce, he is a specialist in, among other things, small businesses.

Starting your own business has been ingrained in the American dream for 200 years. It is an immigrant's passion, a chance to be your own boss, to control your own destiny, to create your own fortune.

Since the 1950s, a kind of immigrant has discovered Phoenix. Its population has grown from less than 200,000 to about two million. What was once a city of 17 square miles is now a community of more than 400 square miles.

Phoenix is now the country's ninth largest city, and

among its citizens are a considerable number of new millionaires, people who have made it on their own.

That's the dream, of course, to make big bucks in your own business. Curiously, in recent years as the dream has become a reality for thousands of Americans, what has acquired almost as much glitter is the idea of having your own *corporation.*

The corporate form has assumed almost magical qualities, as if the corporation itself will assure prosperity. At the least, it will provide spectacular tax benefits. It will somehow enable you to walk away with bundles while paying almost no taxes at all.

None of this public perception was altered by the Tax Reform Act. The act did affect small incorporated businesses in a number of ways, as we'll see, but not radically.

The fact is a corporation may be a completely inappropriate legal entity for a business, especially a new one. But if it fits, it might indeed provide considerable if not magical tax benefits. It is a legal form into which you can pour a number of substantial tax benefits, just as many people imagine. What is interesting is that to a large degree those benefits are not what most people think they are, and they evolve in ways most people are not aware of.

Barely Legal Beauties

For example, so many of the people who go to Bill Raby for help in creating their new businesses have a mistaken sense of the semilarcenous side of "having your own corporation."

The marketing director who is setting up his marketing consulting business says something with a lilt and a question in his voice about an office in his home. And it is true that if he has his office in his home, sees clients there, uses that space exclusively for business purposes, meets a number of other requirements, he will be able to deduct a number of expenses connected with the house.

If he uses, say, 15% of the house for his business, his business may deduct 15% of the common expenses that go with the house: mortgage interest expense paid to the bank, real estate taxes, heat, electricity, other maintenance expenses, including even those for a security and alarm system. Certainly the phones he uses for his business are deductible, and perhaps a portion of others he shares with his family. These are all deductions in addition to his normal direct business expenses, like what he spends for a secretary or stationery.

He may hire his wife to work for him, and so long as he pays her roughly what he'd pay someone he hired in the open market for that job, he'll have no problem with the IRS. It's one way of keeping more of his earnings in the family. If his business is not incorporated, and he does hire his wife, he will even enjoy a special benefit: he does not have to pay a Social Security tax on the wages he pays her. Similarly, he can hire his young children, perhaps as messengers or file clerks, and pay them the going rates. No Social Security tax for their earnings either, and he gets a job done while the business helps to build up their college funds.

So far as his office in his home is concerned, he will also be entitled to that magical deduction for "depreciation." According to the law, he is depreciating 15% of the house, so he will be allowed to deduct that portion of the cost of the house, not including land, each year for 31.5 years. This is true even if in fact because of conditions quite beyond his control, like a general appreciation of real estate values in his neighborhood, the actual value of his house during that period increases many times.

Also, he'll now be entitled to a deduction for his car.

Your Own Corporation: A Shell Full of Tax Benefits 83

There are rules for all these deductions, needless to say, but essentially he will be using his car more than 50% exclusively for business, and can prove it, so he can deduct the business portion of his expenses for running it and possibly depreciate that business portion of the car purchase price over five or seven years, depending on the cost of the car.

Not only will he be entitled to those goodies, but he envisions trips to distant and exotic sales conferences in wonderful spots like Maui, with every penny written off for him and his wife.

Within limits, he's right. If it's a legitimate business conference, and there is as much business reason for his wife to go as he, then he and his wife might indeed have a nice tax-deductible trip. One thing is for sure: He certainly won't have to worry, as he used to, about getting the approval of the head of his company to go to any such sales conference. He is, after all, his own boss.

And, if such a conference occurs in Miami in January, where his 80-year-old mother now lives, he is free to visit her when he's not at the meetings, and maybe they can arrange their visits poolside.

Of course, he might have to show proof and documentation to an IRS agent for all the expenses connected with such trips if he gets audited.

This is all part of the mystique of having your own business, your own corporation.

To a degree, the mystique holds up. But in fact it is small potatoes compared with the real benefits of a corporation for new small businesses. They are to be found elsewhere, usually with the guidance of a tax pro like Bill Raby. And in the end, they matter much more than a "free" trip to Hawaii.

At First, Perhaps No Corporation Necessary

A few years ago young Dr. Thomas Detweiler went to see Raby because he thought it was time to get himself incorporated. He was starting out as an obstetrician/gynecologist and everybody he knew in his field had a thing called a *p.c.*, a professional corporation.

Raby sent him away empty-handed. The fellow didn't need to be incorporated. Starting out, alone in his work and business, there was no need, Raby told him, to incur the expenses of setting up a corporation.

It's not a fortune, but there are legal fees attached, and a certain amount of additional paperwork, mostly state forms, to cope with.

Well, what about all those deductions he'd heard about, all those business expenses?

No problem. He was still entitled to every single one of them. None of that would change. All that would be different, Raby assured him, was the form in which he would be conducting his business.

He would work as a "sole practitioner," a self-employed taxpayer. He would keep track of all his business expenses, whether they were for an office in his home, a medical convention in Chicago, or an X-ray machine, and they would all be taken as legitimate business deductions. To put a fine point on it, they would be reported on Schedule C rather than Form 1120, the form used to report corporate activities, when it came time to pay taxes.

Young Dr. Detweiler nodded but was uneasy. He was worried about a pension. How could he put money aside if he was not incorporated? He apologized for sounding greedy, but gynecologists he knew put tens of thousands of dollars every year into their pension plans, or rather the plans their corporations had, and here he was, not even going to have a corporation.

Not yet, Raby told him, nor was it very likely that he'd have tens of thousands from his new practice to fund a retirement plan. He was on the right track, but that along with the corporation could all come later.

For now they'd set up a Keogh plan. He could put up to $30,000 a year into it—15% of all his earnings or $30,000, whichever was less. Deduct every penny, so none of it would be part of his taxable income. Nor would any of it be taxable until he started to draw it out, which could be any time after he was 59 1/2.

Meanwhile, it could be invested in any number of ways —stocks, bonds, mutual funds, all sorts of investments— earn money for him year after year, and not be taxed at all until he took it out. In his case that would mean about 30 years of tax-deferred growth. And, if and when they set his practice up in a corporation, the Keogh could be rolled over into his new retirement plan, or they could let it grow on its own.

Dr. Detweiler was enough of a professional to trust another professional. Though he felt slightly rejected when he left Raby's office that day, a bit disappointed that he wasn't going to get his own corporation like the big guys, he knew Raby made sense.

With Two, It's Time to Incorporate

He went about his work and did very well indeed. Phoenix, not surprisingly, is a fine place to start an ob/gyn practice. In fact, he reached a point not uncommon with people in his field where the practice was beginning to overwhelm him. There were more patients than he could reasonably handle. Given the nature of that kind of work, which is to say given the nature of nature, he was always on call. Whenever a delivery was to be made, it was to be made. Though he was beginning to prosper, he looked around for help.

He found it in Dr. Juliet Thurow, another young obstetrician/gynecologist who wanted to put some controls on her practice. In addition to maintaining a full practice, she was a determined mother, determined not to let her work keep her from being a good mother to her four-year-old daughter or a good wife to her husband.

They decided to merge their practices. There were certain cost savings they knew they could make, sharing one receptionist/secretary, sharing equipment. But more importantly, they could share themselves. They established a rule for all new patients: The patients had to accept them both as doctor. In other words, when a woman came in for a checkup, whichever doctor was in the office that day would handle the checkup. The same when it came time for delivery: whichever doctor was on duty in the hospital or on call then would deliver the baby.

When Dr. Detweiler and Dr. Thurow spread out their plans for Bill Raby, he recommended they form a corporation.

Adding a partner changed things, he told Dr. Detweiler. To begin with, there were good reasons that had nothing to do with taxes to work through a corporation.

Limiting Liabilities

First of all, a corporation will put some limitations on the exposure to liabilities for each of you. You'll sign a lease for office space, and that should be between the corporation and your landlord. You might need to lease equipment. That should be a contract between the corporation and the company leasing the stuff. Wherever possible in matters like that, neither of you should be personally responsible.

Having a corporation won't protect you from your greatest liability fear, a malpractice charge. There the law won't allow you to hide behind a corporate wall. However, if one of you is sued for malpractice, the corporation should protect the other's personal assets from being at risk if the case is lost.

Though this wasn't going to be so important in their arrangement, still, setting up a corporation would give them a clear record of their relationship. Raby told them of partnerships he had seen where each partner had a different idea of what he owned and what he was entitled to from the business. There was no corporation, nothing but a handshake between them. That can be manageable, so long as everything goes well. But like a marriage that comes apart, when that happens with a handshake business there are big problems sorting out the remains.

Being doctors, they were probably more familiar with medical insurance plans than he was. There were two aspects, however, he would mention as especially meaningful and that their new corporation would pay for.

The Corp Pays Medical Bills: No 7.5% Floor

First, their general coverage for medical reimbursement was more valuable than ever these days. It used to be that medical expenses could be deducted by individuals from their income. Today that is allowed only to the extent that those expenses exceed 7.5% of their income. If you earn $100,000, only the amount that is more than $7500 may be deducted. For most people, in other words, the medical deduction is a fond memory. But with the corporation covering their expenses and those of their families, they wouldn't have to worry about the high deduction floor.

Second, their corporation can pay for disability insurance, an important and very costly coverage for a professional. If one of them is incapacitated, obviously the financial blow is terrible. Disability insurance can cover at least a portion of the income that would otherwise be coming in, but many individuals who are self-employed and working without a corporate umbrella go without it because its premiums are so costly; they don't want to take that much out of their own pockets. But both doctors can be covered with the corporation picking up the bill.

Getting a Little Fancy

All of this was interesting to both of them, but they wanted the juicy stuff. There is probably no profession in America that gets bombarded with more magazines and newsletters dedicated to taxes and money management than the medical profession. Go to a medical conference, and at times from the earnest conversations in the halls and over meals you'd think you'd taken a wrong turn and stepped into a gathering of financial planners.

These two doctors, as serious as they were about their professional work, were avid readers of *Medical Economics, Money, Inc.*, and several newsletters. Retirement plans? they asked, warming to their subject. Deferred comp?

Indeed, these are two aspects of corporate existence that can bring much sunshine into any life.

As Raby told them, such possibilities are rich ones for them because of the considerable control they would have over their corporation with just the two of them as partners.

Though they might have gotten the impression from some of their colleagues that a corporation is a license to do anything, there are in fact plenty of laws and limitations. But still, within those, they could tailor make plans to suit themselves and in the process save themselves substantial tax dollars.

If You Don't Need It Now . . .

First, there was the whole matter of deferred compensation. Judging from the information they had given him, Raby told them that they should each be able to draw about $200,000 a year from the corporation, after funding their $30,000-a-year retirement plan.

If they took that much, it would be ordinary income and taxable at the highest rates. In 1988, that would be 28–33% for federal income taxes, on top of which they would have to pay state taxes, which in Phoenix would amount to around another 6%.

Before the Tax Reform Act of 1986, they would each be facing a top bracket of 50%, plus state and local taxes. So they were now, forgetting for the moment certain deductions they used to be allowed that were no longer available, better off.

But they might be even better off, Raby told them.

Perhaps they didn't need to take as much as $200,000 a year out of the corporation.

Perhaps they could live the way they wanted on, say, $150,000, especially Dr. Thurow, whose husband earned $90,000 a year as the number-two person in a local furniture manufacturing company. Dr. Detweiler's wife taught disturbed children, tough work for little pay: $17,000 a year.

The "Unqualified" Plan: A Rabbi Trust

But, if each of them could take less than $200,000, then the corporation could establish something called an *unqualified deferred compensation plan,* as distinguished from the "qualified" plan in which they are putting $30,000 a year.

A trust would be set up, called a *rabbi trust* after the first such plan on which the IRS ruled, which was created by a synagogue for its rabbi. Each year an agreed-upon amount of money would be put into it. Maybe $25,000, maybe $50,000, whatever would suit their purposes, provided the compensation being deferred was determined in advance of the services being rendered. Since neither of them actually receives the money—it passes instead from the corporation into the rabbi trust—it would not be considered taxable income to either of them until he or she took it out of the trust.

And it couldn't be taken out until certain conditions were reached, normally, on retirement, death, or a state of disability, all of which would be spelled out in the deferred comp agreement between the corporation and each of them.

A bank would be the trustee, investing the money the corporation deposits into the trust each year. While the investment income from the trust would be taxable, the tax would be on the corporation, not them personally. And those taxes, as we'll see shortly, could be extremely low. A corporation has to pay taxes on only 20% of any dividend income it receives. It's one good way of controlling your life's cash flow, Raby said, though there could be a worry. This deferred comp is retirement money, and you want it safe and sound until you need it. However, if your corporation got into deep financial trouble, maybe a malpractice situation, and insurance didn't cover sufficiently, then the funds in this trust could be vulnerable to the judgment creditors.

However, Raby told them, it might be possible to draft the trust agreement so that under dire circumstances for the corporation the assets might be released to you two before the judgment creditor gets to them. A gray area in tax law, Raby allowed, but possible. And they might also have to check with their lawyer on how the bankruptcy law could affect them.

One other consideration with deferred comp. Since the

new law lowered top personal rates from 50% to 28-33%, under some circumstances it might be better not to defer. Take the additional compensation, pay the tax, and invest it yourself. In the long run, you might be better off, and if the rates did go up, you would have taken the income when the tax bite was at its lowest and not face higher taxes when you finally do receive the accumulated income.

For each of them, the decision of what was best would wait until they were ready to enact a deferred comp plan, and then Raby would have to examine their complete financial and tax profiles to decide.

A Larger Step: The "Qualified" Plan

One alternative that would remove the creditor from retirement's door, Raby told them, is some kind of "qualified retirement plan." The Keogh that Raby had set up for Detweiler earlier is such a plan. (States differ in how they treat retirement plans and creditors. In 1987, Arizona, for example, passed a law that protects such funds in qualified plans from creditors. But once you withdraw the money from the fund, a creditor may try to place a claim against you personally.)

Qualified means the plan meets a number of requirements in the tax law, but by doing so it offers special tax benefits.

Unlike a simple deferred compensation plan, with the qualified plan the corporation gets a tax deduction for any contribution it makes to the plan, up to certain limits.

The earnings from the plan go untaxed until you withdraw them.

And again, with their neatly manageable two-person corporation, these plans can be cut to suit their particular needs.

Generally speaking, your corporation might have a defined benefit pension plan, Raby explained, or a defined contribution plan. (For more on these and other retirement plans, see Chapter 10.)

As the name suggests, the defined benefit plan establishes an amount you will be paid year after year when you retire. It might be for $2000 a month. It might be equal to, say, 60% of what you earn during your last five years in the plan.

Once the desired benefits are agreed upon, an actuary figures out how many remaining years you have to work, for how many remaining years contributions to the retirement fund can be made and will have to grow and at what rate of return, how many years you and possibly your spouses will live, and then calculate what amount of contribution the corporation will have to make each month so that the benefits will be waiting there.

And the law permits quite substantial benefits, up to $90,000 a year, adjusted for cost of living. That means, obviously, that to create a fund substantial enough to yield that level of benefit, the corporation and you individually will have to pump large amounts into the plan each year, much more than the $30,000 Keogh limit, if you are into or past your mid-forties. But the more pumped in, the less taxable income for you and the corporation that year. Of course, all of that must be factored into your overall needs. The retirement plan can't drain you to a point where your current standard of living seriously suffers.

The defined contribution money purchase pension plan is a simpler instrument. The corporation agrees to contribute a defined percentage of each employee's earnings each year. It is more suitable to a company with a number of employees.

If you expand your corporation, bring in other doctors, you might want to offer both plans.

Among the laws that have to be observed, you can't have a plan that is "discriminatory," which in other words offers you two special retirement benefits not available to other employees. But those rules can be dealt with as your company expands, if it does.

You might be able to expand the value of the retirement fund by restructuring your working agreement with the hospital where you both serve.

Instead of being hired as individuals, you would now have an agreement between the hospital and your corporation, with all checks made out to the corporation.

But those earnings would be available in calculating your retirement benefit base, which determines the amounts the corporation may contribute and deduct.

The Corporation Lives and "Accumulates"

After sketching out the retirement possibilities for them, Raby said he assumed they would probably next want to hear about accumulating earnings within the corporation.

They looked at each other with surprise and smiles. Here was one they hadn't heard about.

Raby assured them it might become a big reason for them to love their corporation.

This plan, he told them, like the others he had been discussing, depended on their being able to leave some earnings in the corporation, on their not having to draw everything out to live on.

He was thinking of, say, $25,000 a year for each of them.

If that amount could be left in the corporation, they could enjoy various tax benefits.

First of all, if they drew it out as salary, again it would be ordinary income, taxed in 1988 at 28–33%.

But if it remained in the corporation, the tax on it would be only 15%, the corporate tax rate on its first $50,000 of earnings. That would be a tax saving to them of 13% or $6500.

New Law Confusions

Dr. Thurow was puzzled. She had the impression that the 1986 Tax Reform Act had, for the first time ever, dropped tax rates for individuals below those of corporations.

And she was right. But what many lost sight of, Raby reminded her, was that the shift applied to the highest brackets. In other words, corporations were now at a highest bracket of 34%, while most individuals were at 28%. It had been a maximum of 46% for corporations, 50% for individuals.

The shift was so dramatic that at first everybody seemed to be saying, analysts were writing, probably in Dr. Thurow's favorite newsletters, that everyone should change strategies. Don't leave anything in the corporation anymore; take it out. You'll pay less tax on it as an individual than you would through your corporation.

But when you look more closely, what you find is a corporate rate of only 15% on the first $50,000 of taxable earnings.

For her and Dr. Detweiler that meant they could leave it in and avoid sending the government $6500.

Not only that, but that $25,000 could be invested by the corporation in a way that could yield another tax saving.

Corporations, Raby reminded them, pay taxes on only 20% of their dividend income. So, if you figure that it will have to pay on only 20% and even that at a rate of only 15%, you can see there will be very little tax at all to pay on those investment returns.

If, on the other hand, you took the money as salary in order to invest it, you might first be hit with a 28–33% tax on the $25,000, and when you invested the balance you could face another 28–33% on its earnings.

There are limits on the amount the IRS will let you accumulate in the corporation before it hits you with penalties. But for a personal service business like theirs, Raby told them, they could accumulate up to $150,000 before there would be any question, and that amount was unlikely for them for quite a few years.

When they hit that $150,000 ceiling, they would want to take another hard look at a deferred comp plan like the rabbi trust, which could help justify ever greater accumulations.

The accumulated money could also be useful to them as they grow. They might need new equipment, want to fix up their offices, install new and better computers.

The accumulated fund could be tapped for that, and they could save the borrowing costs the bank would charge them.

A Thing Called S Corp

It was somewhat apologetically that Dr. Detweiler raised one more point. Raby had already shed wonderfully illuminating light on their new business world. But there was this one other thing he had heard a great deal about when it came to corporations, and just as he always encouraged his patients never to hesitate if they had a question, no matter how foolish they might think it was, he was following his own advice now. He simply had to know about this thing called an *S corporation*.

Dr. Thurow nodded. She too had heard so much about it, like a wonder drug.

Raby had to smile. You could never underestimate how much the medical world was steeped in business myth and fantasy dressed as advice. Now and then a sophisticated business client raised the possibility of using an S corp, but it was the first time a professional had ever so much as used the phrase.

This was one thing, Raby assured them, they didn't have

to worry about. It didn't apply to their situation. Undoubtedly they had heard about S corps as another of those instant cures that were being prescribed at the end of 1986 when the tax laws were so radically overhauled.

This panacea was related to all that advice to move everything out of your corporation because individual rates were now going to be lower than corporate ones—advice that certainly didn't make sense for them, as Raby had just shown them.

But with an S corporation, everything—gains and losses—passes through to the shareholders, who apply the losses or pay the taxes according to their individual status.

That means no corporate taxes. Whatever the corporation takes in is passed along. The common wisdom was that, since rates for individuals were going to be lower, individuals should be paying taxes, not corporations.

Raby told them that in fact he had reviewed the corporate condition of a number of professional clients in late 1986. Beyond the consideration of the new tax rates, there was another change in the law that made it extremely important for a corporation to rid itself of certain assets like real estate that had appreciated before January 1, 1987, or the corporation could be hit with a big gains tax when the assets were sold after that date.

But in the end, he said, there were not many conversions to S corps of professionals who were earning in the $200,000 range like them. Not warranted in his view, despite the common wisdom.

When the Corporation Rents from You

Speaking of real estate, Raby said, he had one last piece of corporate strategy to offer, a strategy used profitably by a number of his professional clients.

Somewhere down the road, he suggested, think about

buying office space for your practice. One of you might buy it alone, or you could pool your capital and buy it together.

Whatever the arrangement, you then turn around and lease the space back to your corporation. The rental price has to be at a fair market value, but given the going rates, that should be enough to cover the monthly interest costs on your mortgage from the bank, perhaps your real estate taxes, maybe a chunk of the monthly maintenance fees if it's part of a condominium.

You as individuals, if we assume you buy it together, will enjoy all the tax benefits. Within limits, you'll deduct the interest you pay the bank on the mortgage, plus the real estate taxes and a portion of the condo maintenance charges. You'll also be entitled to depreciation on the office space, a deduction connected with rental properties they had heard a great deal about.

The deduction limits are part of the new law, he informed them. Before then, no restrictions on such deductions. Now you may deduct your losses up to your earnings on such a rental real estate property, plus another $25,000. He led them through the uses and limits of the $25,000 exemption, explaining that with their high incomes they probably would not be able to use much if any of it. (See Chapters 2 and 3.)

But that might not be an insuperable problem, with the other planning we've been considering, he told them. And there are going to be benefits to some degree from such a strategy, even if the limits apply.

Basically, they will have an investment in a property, the expenses of which will largely be covered by their corporation. They will be receiving tax deductions to one degree or another. They will have office space, presumably very suitable office space, for which their corporation would otherwise be paying rent to a third party who would be enjoying all of the tax benefits. And presumably their property will appreciate over time, so when and if they wanted to sell it, they'd realize a substantial gain on their investment.

Further, if because of the new law limits on their deductions they had losses over the years that they had not been able to apply against their income from the property, or use them against other passive income they might have, they could add them all up at the time of the sale and deduct them from their gain on the sale.

Or, Raby concluded, leaving them with a nice piece of frosting on this confection, maybe that won't be a problem at all.

Perhaps we do all the financing for the offices by refinancing your homes. The new law has restrictions on this as well, and he explained them. (See Chapter 1.)

But if the financing can be managed within the new limits, we can forget all the restrictions on deduction limits and $25,000 of losses, he told them. Everything we've been discussing will be deductible, just the way the interest you pay the bank now on your home for your mortgage is fully deductible. In a way, we'll just be adding onto that mortgage.

Bill Raby had two smiling doctors staring at him.

It should be clear from the possibilities that Raby spread out for Drs. Detweiler and Thurow as well as the other material in this chapter that even if incorporation is not the same as a blank check and a pass to tax heaven, it does offer a considerable range of opportunities for tax planning and tax saving you wouldn't have otherwise.

But up to this point our attention has been on corporations that offer personal services, that start out small and are largely intended to stay that way. The doctors should do well through their corporation, but they never intend to sell stock in it. The same for the marketing specialist going into business for himself.

Your Own Corporation: A Shell Full of Tax Benefits

The corporate picture changes for someone who may be starting out alone but starting in a business that is intended from the beginning to grow and grow, perhaps reach a point where stock in it is sold to the public, or it becomes attractive to larger companies that will want to buy it out.

This kind of enterprise requires different planning, different tax instruments, often beginning with that creature Dr. Detweiler raised in some embarrassment, the S corp.

Let's consider that and other opportunities in the next chapter.

Checklist: Chapter 4

Tax-smart strategies and perspectives for you to consider and discuss with your tax professional:

1. Should you incorporate or rather operate as a self-employed individual?

2. As a self-employed unincorporated individual, you would be entitled to a number of deductions and benefits:
- office in home expenses and share of related expenses from home; e.g., heat, electricity
- hiring spouse and children if self-employed; no Social Security taxes and more of the income from the business kept in the family
- depreciation of the proportionate space of the home used exclusively for the business office as a deduction
- automobile deductible for business use and depreciable trips to legitimate business meetings, conferences

3. For an unincorporated individual, a Keogh retirement plan permits contributions of up to 15% of earnings or

$30,000 in a year as a tax-deductible contribution to the plan. Income earned within the Keogh is untaxed until drawn out at age 59½ or later. Same for qualified corporate profit-sharing plans.

4. With a corporation, deductions are allowed for premiums on medical coverage and very costly disability coverage.

5. If you have a corporation, an unqualified deferred compensation plan permits you to defer income in a given year and avoid the income taxes that year that you would otherwise have to pay on it. The income earned by the deferred comp fund is not taxed to you but to the corporation, but the corporation pays taxes on only 20% of its dividend income. Possibly set up as rabbi trust, it can be a kind of retirement fund. You pay income taxes only when you finally receive the money.

6. Qualified plans. A defined benefit compensation plan allows your corporation to contribute an amount that will provide a defined benefit on your retirement, according to an actuarial formula. This permits very large contributions and deductions by the corporation for people age 45 and up. Also available to self-employed people.

A defined contribution pension plan calls for the corporation to contribute a defined percentage of earnings of all employees each year up to a maximum of 15% of compensation or $30,000, whichever is less.

7. A corporation might accumulate and invest a portion of earnings. Corporate tax on the first $50,000 of earnings is only 15%, and as noted the corporation pays taxes on only 20% of dividend income.

8. Buy office space as an individual and rent to the corporation. The corporation's rent should cover mortgage interest expense to the bank plus real estate taxes and condo maintenance, if any. Deductions for mortgage interest, taxes, maintenance, and depreciation pass through to you as an individual. In other words, provide the corporation with good office space and have the corporation pay the expenses on your investment. On the sale of the property, the gain will be yours.

5
Your Own Corporation:
Starting Small, with Big Plans

Udall is a good name to have in Arizona, even if it's spelled with one *l*. The Udalls have been a large and distinguished family, old by Arizona standards, with various members serving in state offices, and one, Mo, a respected congressman who even had a shot at the Democratic presidential nomination. His brother Stu served as Secretary of the Interior, which many people in Arizona say is the reason their state doesn't have the water problems of other southwestern states.

Respected and well known are two fine qualities for a name, especially when you want to attach it to a chain of stores. And that was what George Udal had in mind when he went to see William Raby in the Touche Ross Phoenix office.

All his life, George had reminded folks that his version of the name had only one *l* and that, thanks very much, they weren't related. Still, he hadn't objected to the respect he got from lower bank officers and the like when he called.

Now he would use this coincidence to his advantage. Not that that was all he thought his idea had going for it.

For several years George had worked in and managed a

photo equipment store. He had learned the business cold. He never went to college, though he took a few night courses in business, but he never doubted his good head for numbers and his good nose for business opportunities.

He had put life into that store. It was a mom-and-pop operation with both Mom and Pop spending less and less time at it, until in the last couple of years George could pretty much run the business as he wanted, provided he didn't change things too much.

Even so, he almost doubled their volume. He dreamed up countless sales promotions, and he worked well with a small innovative ad agency on an imaginative series of ads featuring an actor who was supposed to be "Pop" himself.

However, it was time, he told Raby, to go out on his own. If he stayed where he was, he'd never make any real money or get a chance to use the ideas he had worked out, as his knowledge of the whole field and the potential of the greater Phoenix market grew.

What he had in mind was a series of camera warehouses, Udal's Camera Warehouses. These would be huge supermarkets, located in shopping malls all around booming Maricopa County, in Phoenix itself as well as upscale suburbs like Tempe, Mesa, and Scottsdale, shrines of consumer consumption.

He would go for volume, advertising the lowest prices in the area. "We will match any advertised price of any competitor in Arizona."

He would appeal to younger people, young families, young working people with money to spend. A massive market for camera and related products. He'd seen the studies.

The stores would be designed with them in mind. Open, colorful, soft rock music piped in, and the salespeople would all be young men and women, attractive, extremely knowledgeable about the products. And all of them on roller skates. They'd roll around the warehouse, pausing at bins to answer questions about what was there, what a particular camera could do, and importantly, George thought, what it could not do.

In other words, this wouldn't be just another discount place; it would be a discount place that treated you honestly and respected your intelligence.

"We respect you and your money" would be one of his mottos. This equipment is expensive. We want you to know exactly what you're getting for your money and what you're not getting.

In keeping with that attitude, Udal's Camera Warehouses would offer a solid maintenance service for everything they sold, at the lowest possible prices.

And, though the original emphasis would be cameras, both still and motion, that was just the beginning.

He intended to expand into video: VCRs, television sets, both standard and high-tech.

He also intended to expand into stereo equipment.

Eventually, he even intended to expand into computers.

And everything sold at the best prices, with the best service.

Beyond that he would from the start try to sell by mail. There were cities all over the Southwest without anything like a modern camera/video/stereo/computer outlet, and what did exist was the usual mom-and-pop operation, out-of-date and overpriced. Through various kinds of advertising and direct mail promotions, Udal Warehouses would try to tap deeply into that potential market.

He had absolutely no doubt about the richness of that market, like tapping into a great, barely discovered oil field. He needed help in how to get to it, starting with how much it all would cost. He was confident that he knew this business and equally confident about what he could do in this venture. But there was a lot about getting off the ground he realized he didn't know.

An S Corp, Perfect to Get Launched

Raby liked the idea and the energetic, imaginative young Udal. He told him that Udal would have to provide him with the basic data so they could figure out what this business would actually require to start, though they could approximate for the moment. Udal assured him he had most of what was needed.

In terms of structure, Raby told him, they should set up an S corporation. It was created for people like him.

Essentially, this was a corporation with some special provisions, which Congress put into the tax law in 1958 in fact to help start-up situations.

Most importantly, an S corp passes through all of its gains and losses to its stockholders.

That one provision can transform a new business from a terrible risk to an attractive investment.

Since 99% of all new businesses have a launching period during which they lose money, those losses are passed on to its investors. And the investors in turn apply them against earnings they have from other sources.

The Tax Reform Act of 1986 puts some limitations on the uses of those losses. For outside investors who are not actively engaged in the business the losses would be considered passive, and they could be used to offset only passive income. Perhaps the investor had such income from another company he had invested in and where he also took no part in the management. But unlike pre-1986, he could no longer apply those losses against active earnings such as salary he took from his own company.

If he couldn't make use of the losses in the year he received them, he could carry them forward indefinitely and apply them when the opportunity was available. If not sooner, then they could be applied against any gains he realized when he sold his share of the company or the company itself was sold.

Heavy Losses plus Increased Basis Equals No Taxes

However, insofar as the losses were concerned, the new law would not affect their value to Udal, the owner/manager. Since he would be actively involved, materially participating in the running of the company, they would be active losses for him and applicable against any other earnings he and for that matter his wife had.

In a sense those losses would be assets for him.

Now, one of the rules with S corps is that you may absorb losses only up to the amount you invest in the company, what is called your *basis* in the company.

Udal told him that he had $50,000 to invest and roughly figured he'd have to raise another $100,000. If possible, he'd like to do it with a bank loan, rather than diluting his company right at the start with investors.

Raby nodded. If you take that approach, he advised, then you should try to get the loan on a personal basis from the bank, and you turn around and lend it to the company. Then you'll have a basis of $150,000 and be able to take up to $150,000 worth of losses and apply them against the salary you draw from the business and any other earnings you or your wife might have.

Udal was delighted. At the beginning, he was not planning on drawing that much out in salary anyway. Same for his wife. And his children, who would be working on weekends and holidays. What that meant, he realized, was that they could go for years without paying any taxes.

The objective of his venture, however, Raby reminded him, was not to cut taxes but to earn money. So looking ahead, what Raby could envision was a period of two to three years of start-up losses, during which time the company remains an S corp. Then there should be a stretch showing some modest profits, though the kind of business that Udal has in mind will probably require an extended stretch of expansion, where each store will drain the profits being generated by the other existing stores. Each new one, in other words, will require its own start-up capital.

By the way, Raby added, as you open these new stores, you might want to think about having a separate corporation for each with the person you select as store manager investing something. It's not the same as franchising, but it could give you capital and them a great incentive.

Also, since they'll be actively managing those stores, they will be material participants just like Udal, and they won't have to worry about the new passive-active restrictions on applying losses. They can take full advantage of them.

Stock Options to Avoid Passive Losses

Another approach to financing the stores could be from passive investors, but if they can't make use of the losses on a current basis, and they are not happy with the idea of carrying the losses forward, Udal could give them debt plus stock options in the company. He continues to own all the stock, but in exchange for their investments they get debt convertible into stock. (Interest paid on the debt is deductible by the corporation.) Then down the road, when the company becomes profitable, or he plans to take it public, they can exercise their options. That way they can realize a nice return on their investments but not be concerned with passive losses.

However the expansion is handled, Raby continued, there should be a point when the business overall will be generating sufficient profits so that we'll then want to convert from an S corp to a C corp. That will permit you to accumulate a certain amount of money within the corporation.

Before the Tax Reform Act of 1986, when individuals paid much higher taxes than corporations, that conversion from S to C corp came fairly early in a company's life. Today, with corporations paying more than individuals at the highest levels, when and why you convert is a matter of finer tuning. Also, you can't keep hopping back and forth. Once you convert from an S to a C corp you must wait 60 months before reverting. But there are reasons, capital accumulation among them, that argue for changing at a certain point.

He then spread out for Udal the strategy of retaining some $50,000 a year in the corporation on which the corporation would be taxed at only a 15% rate (as opposed to 28%) and which the corporation could then invest on a tax-preferred basis, the same idea he had suggested to Drs. Detweiler and Thurow.

Udal told Raby that his instinct had been right. He had been sure there were so many possibilities he didn't even know about, had never heard of. It would have been so easy to start this business the wrong way. Now he thought it was going to be even better than he had dreamed.

Closely Held Corporation

What was evolving with Udal's plan was a closely held corporation.

This is a corporation which is not traded publicly, and does not report to the Securities Exchange Commission. It is commonly found in family businesses, where one, two, a handful of family members own all the stock and control everything the company does.

The form evolves quite naturally. Just as Udal was planning, at the beginning everyone in his family will work for the new company, for minimum wages, Saturdays, Sundays, nights, and holidays.

The business becomes a family crusade, and eventually, in the happy scenario, the sweat and faith pay off. The business becomes profitable, everyone benefits, and because it is all in the family there are potential tax benefits that are unique to the closely held.

Before 1986, for example, there were ways to shift income within a family from the high-bracket parents to the low-bracket children with the family's closely held business as the conduit. Income could be paid to the children-shareholders, and since they normally had little if any additional income, whatever they received from the company was their entire gross income. With only that for income, they would be in a low tax bracket, very low compared to that of their parents. They paid income taxes at their own low level and saved the family serious tax dollars over what would have to be paid if the parents drew the money out of the corporation, paid taxes, and then passed it on to the children.

The Tax Reform Act changed that to some degree. Now children under age 14 pay taxes on their unearned income at their parents' highest rate. So, if the parents are now paying 28%, that will be the young child's rate, with an exclusion for the first $1000. Over 14, the rate is unrelated to the parents' rates. Whatever it works out to be for that child, it is. So for them, income shifting via the closely held family business is still viable. (See Chapters 6 and 7 for more on income shifting within the family.)

When There Is Trust in the Family

There is nothing that guarantees that a family in business together will love and trust each other. Witness "Dallas," "Falcon Crest," and countless other TV dramas built around deceit and greed within a family in big business. Overblown for soap opera purposes, but based in possibility.

But where there is trust, you can take a corporation and reshape it, with extensive tax consequences.

Years ago Raby did that for two parents and their five adult children, all brothers. He broke the corporation into seven corporations with each family member owning 100% of one of those new corporations.

In addition, each owned one-seventh of another corporation that provided services for each of the seven companies.

In order to do that, everyone had to agree to and be satisfied with the share of the pie he or she was now going to own. Since they agreed, the plan could go ahead.

With the separate corporations, each had an opportunity to accumulate earnings, in those days up to $100,000 a year pretax at low tax rates.

Today the low 15% rate on accumulated earnings, as Raby pointed out, would cut off at $50,000. But if you split one large closely held family corporation into eight corporations today, with $50,000 in each, that means a total of $400,000.

The tax on $400,000 for one corporation would be figured at 34%, the highest corporate rate. But split it up, and the tax is only 15% per corporation. You're going to end up saving about $80,000 a year in taxes, which is a substantial amount of money.

The family as a whole will benefit, but again, such a plan will work only if everyone is willing to restructure for the benefit of the family as a whole.

It's not uncommon for family partners to want to go separate ways, sometimes acrimoniously, but in Raby's experience more often for other reasons.

Two brothers who were clients of his, for example, jointly owned a business that was part truck rental and part warehousing. As it happened, one brother had no tolerance for the trucking part of it. People were always getting drunk and smashing the trucks up, and he worried continually about that. Meanwhile, the other brother found the warehouse side of things, while profitable, too boring for words.

So they agreed to split things up. Raby worked out a plan to reorganize, moved the assets around, and created a new corporation. All of the trucks and everything related to the trucking business went into that, along with some cash to balance things out for the trucking brother.

In return, he surrendered his stock in the existing corporation, which left the other brother with 100% ownership of that.

And no tax consequences, which is to say no taxes to pay for either brother, even though the effect was that of one brother buying the other out. If they had parted bitterly and gone through some kind of buyout, there would have been taxes for each, and the whole restructuring undoubtedly would have been costly to both.

Passing the Business On

By the end of his long meeting with Raby, Udal had the general picture of what might be done to be tax smart with his new company when he launched it.

Not surprisingly, he also wanted some idea of what might be done to preserve it.

He was not interested in killing himself for five years to get to a point where he had a company he could sell to someone. This company was to be his life work. With luck he'd succeed, and then, at some point in the future that was hard to imagine just now but that would be there, he'd want to pass this along to his children. That was part of his dream, like the dreams of so many people who start their own businesses.

If you do reach that point, Raby told him, there is also a strategy that could save you possibly millions of dollars in estate taxes.

Most people, Raby went on, know nothing about this part of taxation, but estate taxes can run as high as 50%. (For more, see Chapters 8 and 9.)

If the value of the business at your time of death were passed into your estate, in other words, and you wanted the business to be passed on to your children, there could be tremendous estate and income taxes.

But the law permits an "asset freeze."

Let's say the business is flourishing and you are in your sixties. Your three children are all working hard to make it a success.

At that point we create a new common stock, easily done with a closely held corporation. When we create it, it doesn't have much value. All of the present value of the company goes into redeemable preferred stock, issued to you and your wife in exchange for your common stock. The new common stock we issue to your children.

The present value of the company, then, is in your stock, and that will pass to your estate. If it all goes to your wife, under current law at least, it will pass without any taxes of any kind under the marital deduction. How it is handled within her estate will determine if that estate will have to pay estate taxes.

But all the increasing value of the company, all of the future growth under this plan, goes not into your preferred stock and subsequently into your estate. All of that growth goes to the common stock. Which means that even though the stock is worth next to nothing when your children receive it, 20 years later, when you and your wife die, their stock has increased in value to, say, $15 million.

Since that $15 million does not go into your estate, that $15 million escapes 50% estate taxes completely. It is in the hands of your children. You have kept some $7.5 million within your family that otherwise would have gone for estate taxes.

When and if your children sell their stock, they'll have gains taxes to pay. But they might not sell. They might do any number of things. They might keep it, start making gifts of it to their own children in ways that will hugely cut their own estate taxes and eliminate any income taxes for them on it.

If you want to start your own business and pass it on, you can definitely do it with a minimum of tax pain, Raby concluded.

Asking the Key Unanswerable Questions

Not long after their first meeting, Udal was back in Raby's office. He had brought with him the numbers and other data Raby requested for their projections, and he had also brought a list of questions. The list was on sheets of legal yellow paper under the heading "The Future."

As Udal explained, basically he was so excited by his project, he had stopped sleeping, though that hardly affected his energy level. But night after night he would awake around three in the morning, start thinking about the venture, and that was it. No chance of getting back to sleep for an hour or two.

So, like the good executive he was going to become, he decided to make the most of his time. Thus his list of "The Future."

Basically his thoughts and questions, Raby told him, were quite sensible, if not always answerable. He was wondering about a number of areas that many new businesspeople never thought about. They simply plunged right in, and the lack of any forethought was often costly down the road.

Among Udal's questions were these:

Should we take the company public at some stage, and if so, at what stage?

Every company in America these days seemed to be acquiring or merging. Should we think in those terms as well?

Raby had suggested the possibility of retaining some earnings in the company. Was there more along that line? Should there be an investment plan with the company retaining assets?

What about stock options? One of the reasons he was leaving his present job to start his own company was the lack of incentive. Should his company offer special people stock options? Yet, even as he asked the question, he was concerned about giving up control of his precious creation.

Stay Flexible

Many of his questions, Raby replied, were going to be answerable only after some years, when the possibilities he was imagining became real.

But a general observation: What Udal will be able to do in all of these areas to a large degree will depend on his flexibility. His desire and instinct not to have minority stockholders was important. Though he might be forced to offer stock options to investors, or to branch managers as previously noted, he would be more flexible otherwise. When it came time to decide about going public or merging, Udal himself would be free to make that decision on the basis of what suited his own situation best at the time.

For example, the possibility of merging or selling out. Let's assume, Raby said, that five years from now you've got five stores open, and it's clear that your idea is a good one.

Along comes a major retailer with the same kind of warehouse approach to selling you so admire. They look at you and see themselves in a new business. The approach certainly is consistent with their own, and the company wants to expand.

The Tax-Free Exchange

One possibility is an exchange of stock, yours for theirs. Since theirs is traded publicly, the value is established. Since you think it is an extremely well-run company, you feel comfortable taking its stock, rather than cash, comfortable in the sense that its stock could go down, of course.

But the great advantage in this kind of deal is that there is no tax for you. This is a tax-free exchange. When you go to sell the stock through your broker, you'll pay taxes just as you would any stock. But until that point, no tax. Your gain will be based on the cost of the stock of your old company.

An exchange like that might be the best move in the world for you, but if you have minority stockholders, like key employees, they might not agree.

These employee/stockholders have to stay and cope with the new management, who may or may not want them around. So, you might find yourself drawn into court by these other stockholders in an effort to block the whole deal. And their effort may be enough of a burden and delay that the buyer changes its mind.

So much for flexibility, minority stockholders, and the possibility of merging.

Going Public

Another possibility is to take a trip to Vancouver.

You now get up to 10 stores, and you are hot. Still expanding, you've got the kind of company stock analysts love. They see you as the dynamic entrepreneur you are. They see your idea as a brilliant one that you can soon take national. Ten stores is only the beginning for them. You are a growth company.

So, we go to the Vancouver stock exchange, where they claim they handle small-issue over-the-counter deals probably better than anyone. We make a public offering of the company, which is going to achieve two immediate results.

It will make you a millionaire, or at least make the stock you own worth millions.

And it will give you the financing you need to start a whole new chain of stores in Texas and southern California.

One thing to bear in mind right now, if either of these possibilities—merger or going public—seems at all feasible is to keep good records, use a good recognized professional

CPA firm to do your audits from the start. Because with either of those moves your credibility is being sold.

The matter of stock options and incentives that you raised should be factored into such possibilities.

You're quite right in wanting to offer meaningful incentives to good people. But for a closely held family corporation like yours, it is best if those incentives are not stock.

Again, you want flexibility and freedom to take the company in any direction you please.

Also, if you take someone special in and give him or her stock or stock options, for your kind of one-man operation the idea could backfire.

You could have a falling-out with the person. And off he goes and sells his stock to your competitor, who would love to have access to all your books, which as a stockholder he then could probably do.

Or, if things are bitter enough, he might take you to court. As a minority stockholder he is suing you for violating the law. He claims that you bribed a building inspector, two building inspectors, and he thinks that's a terrible thing and you must be stopped.

On the other hand, you could avoid all that if instead of stock you gave him a special employment contract when he joined the company.

If he's going to be in charge of all the new California stores, then he has a generous bonus formula tied in to the sales in those stores. He has his incentive. You keep total control of your company.

Or, you might have a "phantom stock" agreement. The new employee doesn't receive stock but will receive the benefits that would have gone with such stock.

If you pay dividends, he will be entitled to the amount of money he would have received with X shares. And, if you sell the company or go public, he will receive a proportionate share of that sale. The stock might be worth only $1 a share when he joins the company, but if it's worth $10 a share when we go public, he shares in that growth.

Once again, your important employee has his incentive, while you sustain your control, and unlike the stock option, which may produce no tax benefits for the corporation, the amount the employee receives is fully deductible to the corporation.

Assets in the Corporation

That control can also allow you to determine the corporation's investment plans. There's a world of difference in what it does if you own all the stock.

The retained earnings plan is one possibility. But there are others, and they can throw off considerable tax benefits.

You might reach a point with the business where it is showing profits and a good real estate offer comes to you. There's an office building in trouble. The mortgage is in default, and you can buy it at a very good price. For now, it is throwing off losses. Looking ahead, you think it will appreciate and turn into a good investment.

If your company buys that building, it can take the losses from mortgage expenses, real estate taxes, depreciation, expenses connected with rehabilitating it, and apply them against profits the business is showing from the stores.

To be sure, that is applying passive losses to active income, something the Tax Reform Act allows a corporation to do, but not an individual. Such a use of losses could mean that your company avoids paying considerable taxes.

The question is what happens in the future, if you want to sell the building? How do you get the gain on that sale out of the company into your own hands?

Well, maybe you won't want to. Other things being equal and given a choice, it is usually better to buy an asset like that building on a personal basis. Then it is outside the corporation, and you don't have a tax problem when it comes to getting gains out of the company.

However, if you own 100% of the company's assets, perhaps it doesn't make much difference where the assets lie. They are still yours.

Certainly, after a certain point, there is no need to have the assets in your own hands, as it were. You are not going to spend the money. Raby told him that many of his clients, once they reached such a level, kept enormous assets in their closely held corporations. Deductions from the assets were meaningful within the corporation. And these people weren't concerned about when and how they would get the assets out of their companies.

There were some with deferred comp plans, and periodically they withdrew heavy six-figure amounts from the company in connection with those contracts.

Others were content to control the assets by controlling their companies. If the companies were to be sold one day, the assets could be either part of the sale or spun off. If they were sold, the corporation would then be liable for the gains taxes. If dividends were declared, the corporate client/owners would also face income taxes. But in their planning that was so far in the future that the continued use of the assets over the years rendered the eventual taxes painless.

If the corporations were passed on to subsequent generations, those assets went right along in the generational transfer.

Long Live the Company!
Looking way way into the future, there was the ultimate question on the best way to dispose of a successful company.

In their previous session, Udal had expressed the hope that his three children would want to take it over. If that turned out to be the case, Raby told him they could apply the "frozen assets" strategy, create a new class of stock with all the present value staying in the preferred stock that Udal and his wife would own, and all the growth in the company would go into the new common stock that would belong to his three children. Millions might be saved in estate taxes.

But there were other possibilities, and since they were now trying to anticipate the future, they should think about what might be done if in fact his children were not interested. They wanted instead to be doctors, lawyers, actors and actresses, whatever, but they didn't want to run a camera and appliance business, no matter how successful it was.

Meanwhile, Udal had developed a team of, say, three people who wanted eventually to take over the business and were capable of doing so. In fact, as the years rolled along, they began to get restless. They didn't want to push him out, but they wanted to secure their own futures.

One by one they went to him, expressing their concerns. Hopefully, he would live a long, full life. But by the time he was ready to give up the business, they would be too old to transfer to another company. In other words, if he decided to sell it, they would be out on the street, having given their best years to the company, and while they wouldn't be penniless, they might well have limited resources and no jobs.

The tax law offers a nice solution, the Employee Stock Ownership Plan (ESOP). This is a trust the company sets up and contributes to, with its contributions tax-deductible by the corporation. The team of three top executives and Udal would be the trustees. The trust invests its funds, but the sole purpose is for the trust to buy the employer/owner's stock so that all the employees of the company will eventually own enough stock to control the company.

Year by year, Udal as the 100% owner will sell a portion of his stock to the ESOP and give it an option to buy additional stock upon his death. The trust will take out term insurance on Udal's life, just in case of a premature death. Or it might go to the company's primary bank and borrow money at that point to buy stock from Udal's estate, a loan banks tend to smile upon since the tax law allows them to exclude from their income and thus avoid taxes on 50% of the interest on such loans.

There is even a provision in the Tax Reform Act that until 1992 allows Udal's estate to deduct 50% of the stock it sells to the ESOP from his estate.

Yet another tax break goes to Udal's company. The stock the company contributes to the ESOP is tax-deductible, a welcome break to any company, but for a small company it could be a source of additional financing.

If, for example, the corporation contributes 1000 shares and the value is $50 a share, it receives a tax deduction of $50,000. With the new top rate of 34%, that means it would have available $17,000 that otherwise would have to go in taxes.

If Udal decides he doesn't want to part with all of his stock, he doesn't have to. Perhaps a portion is willed to his wife and children.

But with the other portion, the amount he's selling to the ESOP, he's accomplishing a number of objectives.

First, he's kept his key team together. They know that the company will be theirs to control.

He's also extended his own life with the company. If he wants to slow down but remain a consultant or chairman of the board, his secure team should let him stay on and pay him well.

He has also created a market for the sale of his own stock. How would he dispose of the stock otherwise?

If he decided instead simply to find a buyer for his company, and he decided the company was worth, say, $2 million, did he think it would be easy to find someone to pay him his price?

Even if he got $2 million, in 1988 he'd have to pay a tax of $560,000 on that, so he'd then have only $1,440,000 to invest and produce income.

Alternatively, if he could have that $2 million value continuing to generate income for him, as he could through the ESOP plan, where he would remain an integral part of the company, he'd be better off.

Not only that, but he receives a special personal tax break with the ESOP.

If the ESOP owns at least 30% of the stock after the sale, sales of stock to it are not immediately taxed. He is allowed to take the proceeds of additional sales and invest them, without paying any taxes until he sells the stocks or other securities he bought with the ESOP proceeds.

Udal by this point was shaking his head slowly. Throughout their meeting he had been scribbling notes to himself, less and less as they progressed.

Finally, he decided just to listen. As he said to Raby, he was not there to become a CPA and a tax planner. He was there to absorb the big picture so he wouldn't go on to make expensive tax mistakes out of sheer ignorance.

That was the best kind of planning, Raby replied. All too often, by the time the cases got to him, all he could do was an autopsy.

Checklist: Chapter 5

Tax-smart strategies and perspectives for you to consider and discuss with your tax professional:

1. For a new business with anticipated losses in the early years, consider setting it up as an S corporation in order to pass losses through to yourself and other investors. With

limitations, these losses may be applied against earnings to diminish taxes.

2. With an S corp, bear in mind that losses are limited to the amount of your investment in the company. If you will be starting the company with a loan from the bank, try to make the loan on a personal basis; you then lend it to the new corporation. That increases your investment in it and subsequently the amount of losses you may deduct.

3. If there are separate divisions to the business, as in a chain of stores, think about having the head of each store invest in a separate corporation for that store. That could be a source of capital for the business, and each head would be entitled to S corp losses, then profits. (On the other hand, minority stockholders can provide problems. See #8.)

4. Outside investors who would under the Tax Reform Act be passive investors might not want passive losses. They might instead take stock options that could be exercised when the company becomes profitable or goes public.

5. Review the possibility of a closely held corporation, especially for a family-owned business.

6. An asset freeze is one technique for passing a business on to heirs and escaping potentially millions in estate taxes on the increased value in the company.

7. Try to keep your corporation as flexible as possible, to give you control and the ability to make changes in it as it grows.

8. Minority stockholders can greatly restrict your freedom to change and direct your company. Instead of giving stock for incentives to key employees, consider special employment contracts offering bonuses for specific work performances. Or, a "phantom stock" agreement, which provides the same benefits an employee would receive if he did own stock; e.g., dividends, a return if the company is sold or goes public.

9. In looking ahead, the possibility of merging or selling

out might be effected with an exchange of your corporation's stock with that of another on a tax-free basis.

10. Assets might be acquired and held by the corporation and any losses from them applied against income earned by the corporation. If you own 100% of the corporation, it might pay to keep certain assets in the corporation rather than taking them out for your personal ownership, which would entail corporate taxes and personal for you as well.

11. ESOPs offer a way to pass control of your company to your employees by selling your employer stock to the ESOP trust. The company receives deductions for contributions to the trust. You create a market for your stock, and if the trust owns 30% of the stock after the sale, you receive special tax benefits on your proceeds from sales. In addition, your company continues to operate for your benefit.

6
Income Shifting: Grand Slams, No-Hitters, and the Mighty Cliffords Strike Out

The day after the Tax Reform Act of 1986 was passed by Congress, Robert Zobel, Tax Partner and National Co-director of Financial Planning for Touche Ross, got a call in his Miami office from Sam Lott. Zobel specializes in family tax planning and estate planning, and Sam Lott needed help and relief in just those areas.

Lott said he had read accounts in *The Wall Street Journal*, *The New York Times*, even *The Miami Herald*, but he still couldn't figure out what would now happen to his Clifford trusts. A great deal was at stake. "Did I strike out on both of them?" he asked Zobel.

"You split a doubleheader," Zobel replied, slipping into the baseball jargon that Lott so enjoyed. "Win one, lose one."

He explained that the Clifford trust they had set up for Lott's daughter, Rebecca, would be untouched, since she was over 14. With Lott's son, David, 12, he would still have the Clifford trust; however, its income would now be taxed at a higher rate.

Even that would be bearable. It would be only for two years. During that time, until David reaches age 14, the income from the trust that he receives will be taxed to him at Lott's highest rate, 38.5% in 1987, 28–33% in 1988 and thereafter. Then, after David passes 14, it's taxed to him at his own rate, which presumably will be only 15%.

Lott allowed that that was better than he expected. "When it comes to income shifting," he said, "they dropped a bomb on us, an atom bomb. From what I can see, there's nothing left."

"Damaging," Zobel said, "but not a complete wipeout."

Indeed, throughout the nearly 17 months that the reform act was debated, Lott tracked it closely and was on the phone to Zobel regularly. Lott is a man who looks out for his interests, and he knew he had hundreds of thousands of dollars riding on the way Congress treated techniques for shifting income around a family in general and Clifford trusts in particular.

Lott was a wealthy self-made man who had earned his first fortune on Seventh Avenue by manufacturing a line of medium-priced dresses for large women. (His first wife had a weight problem.)

After selling that business, he went into children's clothes, low-priced knockoffs of expensive European designs. (His two children, Rebecca and David, were born then in his second marriage, and he was appalled at the prices for attractive children's clothes.)

Now, 65, dividing his time between New York and Miami, he was worth several million dollars, which he managed carefully. His attitude toward taxes was they were something that had to be paid, "but only after the last out."

Lott was a great baseball fan, went to every Yankee game he could, and in his view taxes were like baseball. It was the Lotts against the IRS. Each side got its chance to bat, and after nine innings there was a final score. To Lott, he scored every time he and his ace pitcher Zobel could come up with a way to cut taxes within the rules.

Of course, the game was somewhat stacked in favor of the IRS. But even so, Lott never complained so long as he scored a reasonable number of runs.

When Zobel had introduced him to Clifford trusts some years ago, he called them "grand-slam home runs" and "no-hitters" in the same breath.

In fact, they were quite special.

Sections 671–679 of the Internal Revenue Code say to Lott that if he places assets in a trust, unless he meets certain rules, whatever income the trust produces is going to be taxed to him, even if the actual income goes to someone else, say, his daughter or son. This is referred to as a grantor trust.

However, the code also says that if you meet a number of legal and technical conditions, then a trust can become a Clifford trust, and the rules are radically different.

You had to keep the assets in the trust for more than 10 years. It must have an independent trustee. The income had to be distributed annually or at least before the trust terminated. And most importantly, trust income could not be used to satisfy support obligations of the grantor; e.g., food, clothing, education.

But, if those and the other special conditions were met, then the income produced by the trust was *not* taxed at the donor's high rate, but rather at the beneficiary's rate, normally much much lower.

Lott started by setting up a Clifford trust for each of his children, each trust funded with $250,000. As we'll see, these trusts earned income on their investments in a particular way. But their rate of return, which was then some 10% or $25,000 a year for each child, was typical for conservatively invested trusts at that time. (It might be closer to 8% today.)

Lott was in the 50% tax bracket. For him to give each of them that much money a year, he would have to earn $100,000, pay half of it in taxes, and only then be able to divide the $50,000 that remained after taxes between the children.

With the Clifford trust he avoided that. It was the trust, not Lott, who was contributing the income to the children. It was taxed to them at their rate, which in those days amounted to only about $5000 (as opposed to the $25,000 in income taxes he would have otherwise faced).

Lott was able to shift a substantial amount of income to his children free of income taxes to himself, though he would have owed some gift taxes, and provide his children with sizable funds. He was also helping himself in the future. All of the income to the children, which was then invested for them, was giving them funds that increased in value. And all of that income and its appreciation were out of his estate. He would not have to worry about any estate taxes on those funds.

In Lott's case the whole deal was even sweeter. Because he owned nearly all the stock in his successful closely held company, he had considerable clout at his bank. His stock, which represented a major part of his estate, was not readily marketable, however. But it could be used as collateral on a loan, Zobel pointed out to him.

To set up the two Clifford trusts, Lott went to his bank with a plan and his signature, and on that basis the bank lent him $500,000. With that he funded the trusts, making his lawyer the independent trustee.

Then he turned around and borrowed the $500,000 back from the trusts, using the stock of his company as collateral. This was all done very carefully, because there are strict rules about borrowing from a Clifford trust.

But actually the value of the stock he put up was far in excess of the loan.

Further, the interest he paid the trusts was slightly over the going market rates.

With the money he borrowed from the trusts, he paid back the bank.

Once the 10 years was up, he would return to the bank and borrow the $500,000 all over again, take the money, and repay his loan from the trusts.

But a Clifford trust after 10 years and a day may distribute its assets back to the donor, in this case Lott. He would, in other words, receive the $500,000 back from the trusts and return to the bank to repay them once more.

As Lott said: a grand slam and a no-hitter.

- The Clifford trusts were established for his children, each trust worth $250,000, and he did not have to put up a dollar of his own capital.
- He borrowed the capital from his bank and was able to repay it immediately.
- He was able to use the stock he owned of his own company as collateral, and it was legitimate collateral. But the additional benefit to Lott was that there wasn't much else he could do with that stock. It was not traded publicly, and if he wanted to sell it, he would have had trouble finding a market.
- He did have to pay interest to the trusts, some $50,000 a year total. But that was interest on a legitimate loan and so completely deductible by him in those days before the Tax Reform Act of 1986. (Today it would not be deductible interest, although since he incurred the loan before the effective date of the new law, Lott would be able to deduct a portion each year through 1990. Of the interest

paid in 1987, he could deduct 65%; in 1988, 40%; in 1989, 20%; in 1990, 10%; after 1990, nothing.)
- All of the income to his children from the trusts was taxed to them at their low rates. (Again, as noted, that would change for his son under the new law. Unearned income that exceeds $1000 for children under the age of 14 will be taxed generally at their parent's rate.)

A Hidden Asset Clifford

A few years ago Zobel employed some of the same principles in setting up a Clifford trust for a supplier of Lott. Lott decided that the Clifford trust was such a treasure, he would share it with special people only. The supplier, Edward Dreyer, achieved such a status after years and years of business and repeatedly beating Lott's own stringent schedules.

Lott sent him to Zobel; and Dreyer practically whispered the magic word *Clifford*.

In fact, with three children, he could use the instrument, but Dreyer's problem was a lack of cash. Cliffords were fine, but first you had to be able to fund them. Dreyer couldn't, nor did he have the kind of clout with his bank that Lott did.

But he did have a home that had appreciated substantially in value, with not much of a mortgage on it.

Zobel's solution was to make use of a hidden asset.

He had Dreyer refinance the home, take $150,000, divide it up for three Cliffords of $50,000 each. The trusts produced the income for the children, some of which Dreyer invested in zero coupon bonds that were timed to mature years into the future as his children reached college age and would need those expenses covered.

Again, Dreyer himself was spared the taxes on that income, it being paid at the children's rates.

And the interest he paid the bank on his new mortgage was completely deductible by him.

The new law affected Dreyer somewhat differently from Lott. Since he had refinanced his home to set up the trusts before August 16, 1986, all of his interest expense on that would still be deductible. If the refinancing had been after that date, only interest on the amount borrowed up to his purchase price of the home plus improvements would be deductible.

Since all three of his children were over 14, the taxation of income from their Clifford trusts would remain as before, taxed at their rates.

Spousals, the Shrunken Clifford

There was a variation that grew out of the Clifford trust that Zobel once suggested to Lott, but as much as he loved his grand-slam Cliffords, he wouldn't have anything to do with this one.

It was the Spousal Remainder Trust (SRT). It evolved as people began to look for ways to enjoy the benefits of the Clifford trust without the long-term obligations, without having to tie up their assets for a full 10 years.

The SRT was a trust in which, typically, a child received the benefit of the trust's income for, say, four years, enough to cover college.

After that time, the assets could not revert to the grantor, or the income from those four years would be taxed to the grantor. The solution was to pass them to the grantor's spouse. A gift to her would fall under the unlimited marital deduction, which allows transfers between spouses with no income or gift tax consequences. (See Chapter 8.)

Gift taxes on the original grant to the trust were determined by the IRS tables (as were gift taxes for contributions to Clifford trusts), but a grantor could gear his contributions so that they would be covered by his annual donor exclusion of $10,000 per individual.

On the other end, after the four years, the trust's assets all passed to the spouse, with no taxes.

That was the part Lott didn't like. He had been divorced once, he said, and while he loved his present wife, one never knew. And what could be worse than to be divorced from a person and have her receiving tens of thousands of dollars from a trust, for no other reason than that she had once been the legal spouse in a trust plan?

The Big Blow

The IRS never even got to rule on spousal remainder trusts, they were so new. They didn't have to. With the Tax Reform Act, Congress wiped them out.

First went the Clifford trusts. Clifford trusts created after March 1, 1986, would be treated like any other grantor trusts, Congress said. Any income produced by a Clifford trust would be taxed at the donor's highest rate or at the beneficiary's rate in the unlikely circumstance that it was higher than the donor's.

With that, of course, went the whole technique of income shifting. Lott or anyone else could fund such a trust and have it produce income that went to a child. But no income taxes were saved because all of that income would now be taxed at Lott's own high rate.

The same change applied to spousal remainder trusts, which similarly ended their usefulness as income-shifting devices.

Congress further attacked income shifting with a new

provision stating that all unearned income received by children age 14 and under would be taxed at their parents' rates.

This went beyond Clifford trusts, hitting unearned income, interest, dividends, other earnings from investments including capital gains. (An exclusion was allowed on the first $1000 of unearned income.)

The new law did not apply to earned income. That would be taxed according to the child's own tax rate. But if he or she did earn money and invest it, or have it invested for him or her, and it produced unearned income, that too would be taxed at their parent's rate.

Congress did allow Clifford trusts and spousal remainder trusts created before March 1, 1986, to be "grandfathered," to stay in existence and function as they had before. However, even with those trusts the new under-14 rule applied.

That was how Lott "split a doubleheader."

The Clifford trust that was funded for his 16-year-old daughter, Rebecca, could still provide income for her and that income as before would be taxed at her rate.

The other Clifford trust, created for his son, David, 12, would now have all its income over $1000 taxed at Lott's rate, 38.5% for 1987, then 28-33%.

As Zobel told him when he first called, as soon as David passed 14, the Clifford would be as good as old. The income would be taxed to David at his own rate, which would then be 15%.

Meanwhile, there was no denying, as Lott had put it, Congress had dropped a bomb on the whole world of income shifting.

Fighting Back: A Joint Purchase

Lott was a survivor. He had followed the entire tax reform debate with increasing disbelief and dismay. Like countless others, he never believed that Congress would pass anything that was nearly so sweeping and radical as it did.

He was deeply affected in a number of ways, not only in income shifting. The loss of capital gains hurt him with his stock market investments. The passive activity rules hurt him with his real estate investments. The new stricter AMT calculations would cost him money.

But once the dust had cleared, he picked himself up, brushed himself off, and asked Zobel: "So, my friend, what can we do now?"

One suggestion Zobel offered was simple but effective. Lott should put his children to work for him. After school. During the summer. Their earned income, he reminded Lott, unlike their unearned income, is taxed at their rate, not his. And like everyone else, they get the standard deduction. The first $3000 each of them earns is not taxed. Lott would have to pay them at the going rate, but whatever the company pays them is a deductible expense for the company as well.

"Ball four," Lott said. The idea would not work for his kids. They have too much going on with after-school activities. David is a sports freak. Rebecca has gymnastics as well as music. Besides, they don't want to work for their father.

Zobel pitched again. This time he recommended a joint purchase of property with a life estate and remainder interest.

Lott was intrigued, especially since he had never heard of such a creature.

This was a technique, Zobel explained, that might serve Lott's tax objectives and further could fit in with a plan Lott had mentioned not long ago to buy a family vacation home.

With the joint purchase, Zobel told him, you buy the property together with your children.

What you are buying is what's called a *life estate interest* in the place, and your children are buying a *remainder interest* in it.

A life estate is an interest that terminates at the death of the life tenant, you, at which point complete ownership of the property passes to your children.

How much each of you puts into the purchase is based on your age when you buy it, set by IRS actuarial tables. The younger the parent, the longer the tables assume he will live and enjoy the property, the more he pays. A 45-year-old parent would pay 88.56%, his child only 11.442% of the property. At 55, the parent pays 80.046%, the child 19.96%.

Since Lott is 65, if we assume the property costs $100,000, the IRS tables call for him to invest 67.97%, or $67,970. His children put up the balance of $32,030.

That could come from their income funds, which have been growing off the Clifford trust returns.

During your lifetime, Zobel explained, you have the right to use the property just as if you owned it outright.

In addition, if you pay the mortgage interest and the real estate taxes, you deduct them.

When you die, your life interest ceases to exist, and the property passes directly to your children. It does not go into your estate, causing potential estate taxes. All of those taxes are avoided, and the property ends up where you want it anyway.

If the children sell it, they will have to pay taxes on the entire gain, calculated from their $32,030 investment. In other words, they do not get what is called a *stepped-up basis*. They may not assume the full $100,000 value of the property and figure the gain on top of that. They would, if the property were owned completely by their father, it passed into his estate on his death, and then it were bequeathed to them. But the trade-off for not having it go into the estate and be subject to estate taxes is the lower basis.

But if they do not sell it, keeping it until they die and passing it on to their own children at that time, then all of the income tax on the appreciation in the property will be wiped out, although there will be estate taxes to pay on the value.

The same joint purchase approach may be taken, Zobel told Lott, if the property is an income-producing building or piece of equipment.

Only then Lott himself would be entitled to the entire depreciation deduction, and in addition he could be allowed to amortize his investment, yet another deduction.

The passive activity rules would have to be observed, but he could use the deductions to shelter the income from the property.

His children, meanwhile, would be receiving income proportionate to their investment. David's share, unfortunately, would be taxed at Lott's rate, but Rebecca's would be unaffected by the under-14 provision and be taxed at 15%.

"That's right out of the ballpark," Lott declared. "I mean, long gone."

There are several other income-shifting techniques that survived the Tax Reform Act, as we'll see in the next chapter, more suitable to people who earn less than Lott, are worth less than he.

Since circumstances differ, so do strategies. But the long-range objectives of Lott and Natalie Bunshoft, whom we are about to meet, coincide: shift income from high-bracket parent to low-bracket child to deflect and cut income taxes for the parent, increase the financial resources of the child, and eventually spare the parent's estate-punishing estate taxes.

It's a kind of family planning. In the end, it is the family at large that benefits. There's that much more money that stays within the family rather than going to the IRS.

Checklist: Chapter 6

Tax-smart strategies and perspectives for you to consider and discuss with your tax professional:

1. Before the 1986 Tax Reform Act, Clifford trusts were a primary technique for shifting income from a high-bracket parent to a low-bracket child. It was also widely used for shifting income from a high-bracket adult to a low-bracket parent.

Unlike a grantor trust, in which the income from the trust was taxed to the grantor (the person creating the trust), the Clifford trust permitted the trust to produce income that was taxed at the beneficiary's level. A parent in a 50% bracket, in other words, could create the trust. The income from the trust would go to a child in the lowest bracket and be taxed at the child's rate.

To qualify as a Clifford, a trust had to observe special rules, most especially that its assets would remain in the trust for at least 10 years and a day. After that period, the assets could revert to the grantor.

2. The spousal remainder trust evolved from the Clifford trust as an attempt to enjoy the benefits of the Clifford trust without tying up assets for 10 years.

With these, the income from the trust might typically go

to a child for a period of less than 10 years, after which the assets from the SRT were distributed to the spouse.

3. Under the right circumstances, it was possible to fund Clifford trusts with bank loans in which stock from the grantor's closely held corporation was put up as collateral on the loan. Where this could be done properly, the donor might be able to fund the income-producing trusts without using his own capital and further enjoy a double tax benefit: the income received by his child would be taxed at the child's low rate, and the parent would enjoy a deduction from interest he was paying on the loan.

Under the Tax Reform Act, both of those benefits today might be limited or eliminated. The income to the child might be taxed at the parent's rate, if the child is 14 or under. And the interest deduction might not be fully deductible, unless the loan came from a refinancing of a principal or secondary residence.

4. Where a parent wanted to create a Clifford trust but didn't have the assets to do it, the parent refinanced his home and used the proceeds to fund the Clifford trust. Income was effectively shifted to the low-bracket child, and the parent received a deduction for his interest expense on the refinanced mortgage.

5. The Tax Reform Act of 1986 eliminated the special tax provision of Clifford trusts. All Clifford trusts created after March 1, 1986, the law stated, would have income taxed at the highest rate of the donor, not at the rate of the recipient.

Those created before that date could exist and operate as before.

However, they would be subject to another new tax rule: Any unearned income received by a child aged 14 or under would be taxed at the highest rate of the child's parents.

Effectively, then, only Clifford trusts created before

March 1, 1986, and presently providing income to a child over 14 would still yield the old tax benefits.

6. A joint purchase of property with a life estate and remainder interest is a purchase made by a parent and child together of a property.

The parent purchases a life estate interest in the property and the child a remainder interest. On the death of the parent, the life estate terminates, and the property passes directly to the child.

How much each invests is determined by IRS actuarial tables; the younger the parent, the longer the tables assume he will live and enjoy the property, the more he pays.

At 65, a parent pays 67.97%, the child the balance of 32.03%.

The parent has use of the property during his lifetime, and if he pays the real estate taxes, he receives a deduction for them.

If the property is income-producing, the parent is entitled to the full depreciation deduction and may also amortize the amount of his investment, another deduction.

On the parent's death, the property passes to the child and does not enter the parent's estate. Estate taxes on the property are therefore avoided. If the child sells the property, he will face income taxes on his gain, which will be calculated from the amount he alone invested in the property.

But he may retain the property until his death, passing it on to his children. In that case, there would be no income taxes at all on the appreciated value of the property.

7
Income Shifting: Natalie's Quest—Something Big for an Average Person

Natalie Bunshoft said she needed a lot of help from Robert Zobel.

She had just gotten divorced, and for the first time in her adult life she was taking control of the family's finances, not an uncommon situation for newly divorced women.

However, she had something of an advantage over most women who find themselves on their own at age 42. She was a successful businesswoman. She owned a large travel agency in Miami, a business she had built up over the years.

Even though she had a good head for business, she had left most of the financial planning for their family to her husband, a lawyer, who in fact had no particular talents in this area. But again that was a fairly traditional division of family labor, the man assuming responsibility for money matters.

Natalie was not so much anxious over her new responsibility as angry. Only now, when she took stock of everything after the divorce, did she realize what a bad job her husband had really done.

In the area of income shifting, for example, he had done nothing, a very costly omission, Zobel told her.

Unfortunately, they had lost out, he explained, on a number of techniques that over the years might have meant substantial tax savings for them, given that they both were working and earning increasingly well during the 12 years they were together.

That might be so, Natalie allowed, but that was past. With this as with the rest of her life, she wanted to look ahead.

Her big question was, after the new law, what was left? "What's possible for someone like me, an average person who isn't worth millions of dollars?"

She had told Zobel that she drew a salary of $100,000 from her agency, and she could take more, if needed. Her ex was not paying her any alimony but was paying $2000 a month childcare, which was $1000 for each of their children, Allan, 12, and Sam, eight.

Zobel told her that even though the new law wiped out so much in this area, there was a lot she could still accomplish because she was starting while her children were still young.

$10,000 a Year Tax-Free

To begin with, there was the annual gift tax exclusion. Under this, she was allowed to make a gift of $10,000 to each of her sons each year or to anyone—a friend, a niece, anyone—and there would be no tax of any kind on that money. That would add up, and her sons would develop their own funds.

Until they passed the age of 14, if they had that money

invested for them and received income from the investments, the boys would be taxed at her rate, which would be 38.5% on her 1987 income, dropping to 28% for 1988.

But there was a way to avoid those taxes. The boys' money could be invested in tax-exempt bonds. In that case they would have no taxes to pay on the income.

After age 14, which was only two years away for Allan, whatever they earned from their investments would be taxed at their level, not their mother's. So, they could diversify their investments with much less concern about tax consequences. They could earn up to $17,850 and still be in the 15% bracket.

For now you could also "gift" them tax-frees, Zobel suggested, to add to their funds. If these gifts exceeded her $10,000 exclusion, she would owe gift tax. But that could be covered by the Unified Transfer Tax Credit.

The unified credit entitled her to a credit of $192,800, which would cover the taxes on $600,000. So she could gift her sons or transfer assets to them or anyone for a total of $600,000 and not have any gift taxes to pay. (More in Chapters 8 and 9.)

Don't Laugh at Savings Bonds Anymore

Another vehicle that would work well for her and the boys, Zobel thought, were Series EE U.S. savings bonds.

She actually laughed when he suggested them and told him she wasn't that patriotic. It was her clear impression that those things didn't pay anything.

They didn't used to, Zobel told her, but times change. They're much more competitive, paying something like 6–7% interest, guaranteed to pay at least 85% of the return on a one-year Treasury bill if you hold them five years.

And from a tax perspective, they are useful because you

don't have to pay any tax on the accruing interest until you cash the bond in. With both boys, you simply wait until each has passed 14 and then cash them.

Looking ahead, she might want to plan for the college expenses for both boys.

She told him that she and her ex had agreed to share those costs equally.

This was the kind of thing for which a Clifford trust used to be ideal, but alas no more. However, there were two current strategies she could consider.

One was to purchase a single-premium life insurance policy. Though Congress might also change this, these policies escaped the Tax Reform Act.

It was still possible to have a large fund to draw upon tax-free with these policies.

A Loan That Is Not Paid Back

Basically, Zobel explained, you buy a life insurance policy and your premium (net of fees) is divided into three parts. One portion goes for the life insurance coverage, another for the expenses of writing the policy, and the third is invested to build up the cash value in the policy. In some cases you can choose what kind of investment your policy goes into—mutual fund, money market, etc. In others, the insurance company dictates the investment policy.

Either way, if the investments are well made, that part of the policy increases, and it does so without any taxes on the appreciation. Your earnings in there are compounding on a tax-free basis, a great advantage.

You may borrow against this growing fund, and you do not have to pay any taxes on the amount you draw out either. Nor do you have to pay the loan back, although you do have to pay interest and it is not deductible. That means you could end up with a substantial fund to pay college expenses without any obligation to repay it.

There are limits on the amount you may borrow—generally so you don't cut into your insurance coverage—and if you start borrowing too soon, you'll have a high sales fee to pay. Depending on the company and the policy, you'll have to allow the policy to grow five to eight years untouched before you can borrow without any fee, and the amount is often scaled down with the years. You also need to pay premiums in four of the first seven years you own the policy for the interest on policy loans to be deductible.

But it is a way to develop funds for the children that will be essentially tax-free. Usually these policies make sense only if you can use the insurance portion of the policy as well as the cash buildup. And though Zobel and she hadn't yet reviewed that part of her financial profile, he thought it was likely that with two young children so dependent on her the insurance would make sense.

One option with these policies they would also have to think about was insuring the children rather than her, taking the policies in their names.

This would result in much lower premiums, since they would be based on the ages of the children. When the children were old enough, they would borrow from their own policies, and on completion of college, assume responsibility for the policies.

There is a risk with these policies that Congress will eliminate some of their tax benefits, possibly tax the gains on the buildup fund or tax the "loan" you take from it.

The other possibility for covering those enormous college bills is refinancing the home.

The new law put limits on the amount of mortgage interest you may deduct, up to the amount you paid for the home plus improvements or the fair market value of the home, whichever is less.

However, it allowed two specific exceptions over and above that. One is for medical expenses. The other, for educational expenses.

So when the time comes, she could refinance her house and use the money to pay for college. And all of the interest on the loan will be deductible by her. It isn't the traditional form of income shifting, but as a modern adaptation it's a strategy that could help her and her boys.

Exploiting Your Own Business

As Zobel sketched out the various income-shifting possibilities, Natalie Bunshoft in her businesslike way was making notes.

Now she closed her folder and shook her head, somehow disappointed. She was thankful for any and all ideas, she told Zobel. And there was no question she could make use of several of the strategies he had spun out. But still she had expected something bigger.

"Mrs. Bunshoft, nobody ever said the tax law was fair," Zobel said. He told her that when President Reagan sent his proposals to Congress he used the words *fairness* and *simplicity* in the title. Pretty amusing use of language, since out of that came the Tax Reform Act of 1986, which was why she now felt so frustrated and cheated.

That she accepted and understood. But even so, she had the impression that it was still possible to do more.

Zobel assured her they weren't dead yet. Who owns your travel business, he asked her? What form of business is it? Is it incorporated?

She told him it was a corporation and she owned all the stock.

"Then we can do more," Zobel told her. He had two

strategies in mind, one quite simple, the other somewhat complex.

First, he continued, hire your sons. He told her what he had told Sam Lott, but Lott was too wealthy and his children too spoiled to be receptive. Hire the children after school and during summer vacations, other breaks. They can be messengers—a substantial expense for any travel agency—they can be file clerks, clean the office.

Pay them whatever the hourly wage is for the job. If it's $5 an hour, that's $40 a day or $200 a week. Each child could earn $3000–5000 a year, and the first $3000 would be untaxed, the balance taxed only at their 15% rate.

Furthermore, every cent paid to them would be a legitimate business deduction for the travel agency, the same as any other wages the company paid.

She liked that. She could really use them, and she had always wanted them to learn something of her business.

The Family That Plans Together

Zobel's other idea was to create a family partnership.

He asked her a few questions about the offices the agency presently occupied, the equipment it required, what was rented, what owned.

Essentially, everything expensive, like space and computers, was rented. Desks, file cabinets, inexpensive stuff had been bought over the years.

Zobel looked up from his own notes, nodding. He thought this might work, very well indeed.

The plan was to create a family partnership, with Natalie and her two sons the partners. It would be funded, he explained, by all of them. The children's shares could initially come from her, the $10,000 gift she is allowed to make to each child each year without any gift tax.

Income Shifting: Natalie's Quest 147

That's $20,000; perhaps she puts in another $20,000–$30,000 as her own share of the investment, depending on how the numbers work out.

Then the travel business goes out and finds suitable office space for itself that can be bought. And it does the same with the computers it uses and its complicated telephone system, as well as any other office equipment that is now being rented.

Let's say the office space will cost $150,000, everything else another $50,000.

You then go to the travel agency's bank, he told her, where we assume good credit and relations, arrange a loan for the family partnership, which you sign. You'll need $30,000 to put down for the offices and assume another $10,000 toward the computers and the other equipment. A total of $40,000, which the partnership has, $20,000 from the boys, another $20,000 from her.

The bank lends the partnership $160,000, of which $120,000 is a mortgage on the offices, the rest a simple business loan.

Now the partnership owns the property and the equipment, and it leases everything to the travel agency. Everything has to be at fair market value. The rent the agency pays, in other words, has to be what it would pay to any unrelated third-party landlord for those particular offices, and the same for the equipment.

But it should amount to more than enough to service the bank loan, which means the partnership will begin to acquire cash.

Also, the partnership will enjoy a number of tax benefits. It will be able to deduct all the interest it pays to the bank on the loans. It will be able to depreciate the office space and the equipment.

All of those deductions will increase and improve its cash flow, and that money will be going to her and her sons. To some degree, she can control the flow, retaining a certain amount of cash in the partnership. That will allow her to time the flow of cash to her children.

With the new laws, the income from the partnership would be from a passive activity, which might cause some problems for her.

The boys share of the taxable income will be taxable to them. But the plan would permit her to shift an impressive amount of income to each of them, income that otherwise would go from her business to some landlord or equipment-leasing company.

"Why make them rich," Zobel asked her, "when you can keep all that money within your own family?"

That was exactly the kind of "something big" Natalie was looking for.

Helping Parents

There was one other kind of income shifting Natalie wanted to accomplish, if anything were possible.

Her father had died some years ago, and her mother lived in the modest North Miami condo they had owned together. Basically, she existed on Social Security and the earnings from conservative investments that came from the proceeds of two life insurance policies left by her husband.

With about $15,000 a year, the woman was not starving. But she needed all her income to get by. And, rationally or not, being that close was a continual worry to Natalie's mother. Natalie lent her money from time to time, when a Social Security check was late and she needed to pay some bills. And Natalie knew that she would always be able to take care of her mother in that way.

But such sporadic emergency support only made the 76-year-old woman more nervous. From time to time, Natalie used to ask her husband if there was some way they could do something. She wasn't sure what, though she had friends who had worked things out with their accountants for just such situations, and they were friends with no more money than Natalie and her husband had. But this became just one more piece of financial planning that slipped by.

Now, Natalie wondered, since she was trying to overhaul family money matters, what might she actually do?

This was another problem that many people used to solve with Clifford trusts, Zobel told her. It was often a better arrangement with older people, because the law allowed you to set up the Clifford trust for them for the required 10-year period or until the death of the parent. Since the parent would often die before the 10 years, the assets of the trust would revert back to the supporting son or daughter even faster than usual with no tax consequences for them.

Trust for Mom, Remainder for Children

But with Clifford trusts eliminated, Natalie could consider establishing a trust that would provide income for her mother during the woman's lifetime with a remainder interest to her children. In other words, on the death of her mother, the assets of the trust would pass to her sons.

With arrangements like that, there was frequently a concern about controlling the funds. The trust could be set up so the children would not be able to get control of the assets until they were 21, but after that it would be theirs.

A quite different strategy would have Natalie buy her mother's condo from her.

Paying the monthly maintenance charges and the monthly mortgage payment to the bank must be worrisome matters hanging over the woman. Natalie might be able to relieve her of those anxieties in a tax-beneficial way.

Essentially, the plan bore similarities to the one Zobel

had sketched out earlier for the family partnership and Natalie's travel business.

This time Natalie herself would buy the condo, which she estimated would be worth approximately $30,000 on the open market. So, she'd need only about $5000 to put down.

Less Anxiety for Mother . . .

She would then rent the condo back to her mother, and the rental income would go toward paying the mortgage and the other expenses of the condo.

Her mother would be in a new and more comfortable financial situation and be able to handle the rent easily.

She would first of all have a fresh $30,000 invested for herself, presumably returning at least 8% or $2400 a year. That alone would pretty well cover her new rent.

Further, she would be relieved of the monthly payments to the bank on her mortgage and to the condo association for maintenance.

So long as the condo was her mother's principal place of residence—which it would be—and Natalie charged her a fair market value rent, the place would qualify as a rental property for Natalie.

It would be subject to the new passive activity rules as they apply to rental properties, which meant that the expenses and deductions generated by the property would be deductible first against the income it produced and then only against passive activity income.

So, if the income were, say, $3000 a year, Natalie could apply deductions from mortgage interest, real estate taxes, maintenance, and depreciation up to $3000. She would have no income taxes to pay on that amount.

... Big Shelter for Natalie

If there were expenses in excess of that, Natalie had a few possibilities.

If she had passive income from other sources, she could continue to apply the passive losses from the condo project against that income.

Or, since she was presently earning $100,000, her adjusted gross income in all likelihood was going to be between $75,000 and $80,000.

That meant a great opportunity: she would qualify for the $25,000 loss exception. Having less than $100,000 of AGI, she could deduct up to $25,000 of losses from the condo against any other income, including her salary from the travel agency. The condo, in other words, could be a substantial tax shelter for her.

In the future, if her AGI went above $100,000, the $25,000 would be phased out as her AGI rose from $100,000 to $150,000 (as noted in Chapter 3). Any excess losses that she could not apply could be carried forward to future years.

But for now, she could make good current use of the condo's losses. Losses carried forward could always be applied against income from the condo. And when she finally sold the condo, she could then apply all of her accumulated passive losses against her gain on the sale, or against any other income.

There was yet another approach to this strategy that Zobel sketched out for her.

Natalie could buy the condo from her mother, but forget about renting it to her. She would simply let her mother live in the house rent free.

The house would be a second home to Natalie. As such, she would not be entitled to the depreciation deduction, or to write off expenses connected with a rental property. But she would be entitled to a complete deduction for all the interest expense on her mortgage, as well as any local real estate taxes.

Her mother would have the $30,000 as before, and the income from that to live on. Natalie would not have the cash flow from her mother's monthly rent payments, but she would be better off in terms of tax benefits, and she would avoid the complications and limitations of the passive activity rules.

When Is Good, Too Much?

Those possibilities appealed to Natalie, but she confessed to a doubt. She was concerned that she might be taking on a little too much to start. She was thinking about making a gift to her sons each year, plus what she'd have to invest in the family partnership, as well as possibly launching some of Zobel's other strategies. In her head, it was adding up to more than she could handle.

Zobel assured her that first they would do all the numbers, and they could then readily see what was too much. Right now, he was trying to lay out possibilities.

Just so long as he understood, she told him, that she didn't want to relieve her mother's anxieties and end up a nervous wreck herself. Assuming for the moment that she was right, was there some lesser alternative, she wondered, something more modest than buying the condo that they might try for now?

Absolutely, he told her. She might simply give her mother a little money. Maybe the margin we're talking about is, say, $2500 a year. Remember, Zobel told her, you can give your mother up to $10,000 a year with no taxes for anyone. So, maybe you send her $200 a month that she can apply to her ongoing expenses. That's a painless $2400. She can count on that, it's no great strain for you, no gift taxes for you, and she has that much more of a cushion against her money worries.

Perhaps we start out that way, he suggested, and then in a year or two we launch the other plan where you buy the condo from her. But he would like to do all the numbers on that condo and see exactly how much income she would be able to shelter from it. She might well be able to buy the condo from the tax savings alone.

Natalie told him she would sleep on it and they could decide after reviewing those numbers. Whatever they decided, she had to feel comfortable with it.

"No problem," Zobel said. "The idea is to shift income and be as tax smart about it as possible. But like all tax planning, whatever we do must be more than fancy maneuvers on paper. It has to make sense in real life. And you have to feel completely comfortable with it. You have to live with it."

Checklist: Chapter 7

Tax-smart strategies and perspectives for you to consider and discuss with your tax professional:

1. Start shifting income within your family early, when your children are young and you have years to make transfers and allow them to appreciate.

The annual gift tax exclusion is an example. The law permits you to gift $10,000 a year to any child or other person with no taxes for anyone. Such gifts and their subsequent investments can grow impressively over a number of years.

2. With all income shifting, bear in mind that the Tax Reform Act of 1986 established that any *unearned* income over $1000 received by children under the age of 14 will be taxed to them at their parents' highest rate, which could be 38.5% for 1987, 28–33% thereafter.

However, such income taxes could be avoided if the children are receiving tax-free income.

After age 14, they are taxed at their own rates. Starting with 1988, they may earn up to $17,850 and still be in the 15% bracket.

3. The unified credit may be applied against gifts to children that exceed the $10,000 annual exclusion. Each taxpayer is allowed to make gifts up to $600,000 without having to pay any gift tax.

4. Series EE U.S. savings bonds have become useful vehicles for shifting income. They now pay a competitive rate of 6–7% interest, if you hold them five years, and you don't have to pay any tax on them until they mature.

With children under 14, wait until they are over 14 before cashing in the bonds.

5. Single-premium life insurance policies are worth considering as sources of tax-free funds, especially useful for large anticipated expenses like college costs. Presently, the portion of your premium that is applied to the investment part of the policy grows within the policy without any taxes. You may borrow from that fund, within limits, and not be taxed on the amount you withdraw, nor do you have to repay that loan.

6. Refinancing your home is another way of dealing with such large expenses. The new law allows refinancing of your principal residence over and above normal limits for educational purposes. All of the interest on the loan is deductible.

7. If you own your own business or work in one where this is possible, hire your own children for after-school hours and vacations. So long as they perform legitimate jobs—being messengers, file clerks, receptionists—and are paid the fair market wage, they can accumulate income, and the company is entitled to a business deduction, just as it is for any other wages paid.

The first $3000 a child earns is not taxed, and the remainder is taxed at his or her own rate. Further, if it is your unincorporated company, the child's income won't be subject to Social Security or unemployment taxes.

8. A family partnership can be created by members of your family to buy and lease back to your company necessary working space and equipment.

The family members invest in the partnership, the children contributing funds that may have been given them by you as part of your annual $10,000 exclusion.

The partnership, probably with you signing the note, obtains a loan from the bank, sufficient to buy the office space and the equipment required by the business.

The offices and equipment are then leased back to the company at fair market rates.

The partnership receives the rental income, which should pretty well cover the loan expenses, for which it gets deductions. It also enjoys depreciation deductions on the rental office space and the equipment.

9. Income shifting may be planned with parents as well as children.

Though Clifford trusts have been eliminated by the Tax Reform Act, a trust may be set up for a parent, with a remainder interest for a child or children.

The parent would receive the income from the trust during his or her lifetime, the tax on that being paid by the beneficiary.

At the parent's death, the assets of the trust would be distributed to the children.

10. Consider buying the home your parents live in and renting it back to them.

It relieves them of monthly payments on the mortgage and/or maintenance charges if it's a condo or co-op and provides them with a lump-sum purchase price that they can invest. The proceeds will go toward the rent.

So long as it is their principal residence, and you charge them a fair market value rent, the place becomes a legitimate rental property for you.

You may deduct your expenses on the property—mortgage interest, expenses to maintain the home, real estate taxes—against the income it produces.

If expenses exceed income, the passive activity rules would apply.

8
Estate Planning: Does One Size Fit All . . . Almost?

Joan Slater sat stiffly, alone on one side of the large oval mahogany table in the conference room of the Touche Ross office in downtown Miami. She stared off into the middle distance at Biscayne Bay sparkling in the sun out beyond the windows she faced, her head slightly cocked toward the man who sat across from her, George Lehrman. Papers spread before him on the dark burnished surface, Lehrman was their family lawyer. He was reading her husband Jeffrey's will to her.

Listening closely at the end of the table, scratching notes on his yellow legal pad, was Robert Zobel, Tax Partner for Touche Ross, estate and financial planning specialist, and the man responsible for the shape of much that is in the will.

Off in one corner of the room was the "deceased," Jeffrey Slater, listening closely, making his own notes.

It is called a *cold reading* of the will, an exercise used by Touche Ross that enables clients like the Slaters to actually hear what's going to happen to their estates after they have died. While the immediate effect is slightly eerie, the process allows them to be sure that in fact their wills do express their desires, that in fact their estates will be disposed of just as they want.

Throughout the reading, Joan interrupts. There are terms she is not sure of. There are provisions that are unclear.

Since Jeffrey is presumably gone, he is not to speak until the will has been read completely. He waits, but as soon as Lehrman has finished he is on his feet.

"Major question," he says. "Major. Where's the Crummey trust? My life insurance. I don't hear anything about that. Where is that?"

"Don't worry," Zobel tells him. "It's coming. It's in a separate document."

Slater nods. "Okay," he says. "Just that that's important."

Zobel agrees and has to smile. Slater has come a long, long way in the few months since he first walked into Zobel's office. Now he is reminding his lawyer and Zobel that he cares about a Crummey trust, which indeed is important. It will enable his estate to shift assets worth $350,000 into a trust, which will provide income to Joan after his death and will pass on to their children after her death, all with no estate taxes for anybody. But a few months ago, Slater had questions about the necessity of a will at all.

Yet, in his way, Slater was not so unusual. While he was certainly successful in business and not unsophisticated when it came to taxes as they affected the furniture company he worked for, he knew precious little about estate planning and estate taxes.

This is a very complicated section of the tax law, largely untouched by the Tax Reform Act, and most people are unfamiliar with it. Yet the taxes that can result on an estate are much higher than an individual might face on his income during his lifetime. In 1988, they can run as high as 50%. They can also, with some foresight and intelligent planning, often be eliminated altogether or at least greatly minimized.

Who Needs a Will Anyway?

Originally, Slater, 48 years old, had gone to Zobel reluctantly. Though he didn't come right out and say it at first, basically he thought of wills, trusts, and such stuff as fine for very rich folk, who might be able to use them and might also be able to afford the fees that went with them.

He told Zobel in their first session that he did not have a will and really wondered whether he needed one. His desires were clear and simple, and his estate in all likelihood was not going to be huge.

Quite simply, he wanted to leave everything to his wife, age 40, and he assumed that happened automatically. That even without a will, a husband could leave everything to his wife with no taxes for anyone.

Zobel told him he was half right. There is something called the *marital deduction*, which allows husbands and wives to leave everything to each other without any estate taxes. It doesn't matter whether you leave her $10,000 or $10,000,000; there is not a penny of estate tax to pay, Zobel told him.

That's simple. But what happens after she dies?

Slater said he'd want whatever was left of his estate to go to his children.

Fine, Zobel responded, but you won't be around to see that that happens.

Slater assured him that was no concern. He and Joan had talked about this, and they see it the same way. After all, they both love their children.

Providing for the Unexpected

Zobel raised a few possibilities Slater had never considered. Suppose by the time your wife dies her feelings about your children have changed?

Or, suppose she gets very religious after you die and decides to leave everything to her church instead of to the children?

Or, as often happens, though it's tough to imagine right now, suppose she remarries, and she decides to leave everything to her new husband?

"My money?" Slater asked with a touch of surprise and alarm in his voice.

"Has happened."

Slater thought it over and told Zobel he now understood why he needed a will, to keep that kind of thing from happening. He loved his wife, but he was not supporting any second husbands.

That was only part of it, Zobel told him. If Slater wanted to be sure that his estate got treated according to his wishes, and he wanted to cut his estate taxes to a minimum, then their estate planning had to start with a will.

To begin with, Zobel told him, if he doesn't have a will he dies intestate, and the state can intervene. Different states have different laws for dividing up estates that are not covered by wills. Slater might want everything to go to his wife. But he might die residing in a state that says only one-third goes to his wife, one-third to his brothers and sisters, the balance to his children.

Zobel told him of a client who had been divorced but had never changed his will. He intended to, indeed had a clear idea of what he wanted to leave to whom: The great bulk of the estate was to go to his present, second wife, small amounts to the three children from his first marriage, larger amounts (though still within the $600,000 tax-free exemption equivalent the law allows him) divided between the two children from his second marriage. Not a penny to his first wife.

All quite clear, but he was a terrible procrastinator. For three years, he told Zobel he simply had to get a new will drawn, and then one day at age 52 the man had a heart attack, and that was that. He looked to be in great shape, never drank anything more than the occasional glass of white wine, a jogger, a very careful eater. Ironically, perhaps because he did take such good care of himself, he never felt much pressure to redo that will.

No Updated Will, No Control

At any rate, his will when he died still referred to his first wife and his three daughters from that marriage and didn't say a word about his second wife or their children.

The estate was worth about $12 million, and in some states all of that might have been distributed just as the old will stipulated, leaving his second wife and their children with nothing.

To a degree, the man was lucky. His state at least recognized the validity of his divorce decree, so it distributed half to his second wife, the balance to the son and daughter from their marriage. Which was better than it might have been. Yet the children had to pay a lot of estate taxes, which could have been avoided. His second wife didn't end up with what he really wanted for her. Indeed, no one ended up receiving what he had in mind because he never said what he wanted in a revised will.

So, you need a will, Zobel said, and you need it to be current. Without a will the estate could be tied up in probate court by the state's process, as the beneficiaries sort out who gets what. An estate generally has both probate and nonprobate assets, the latter being assets that pass directly to someone without having to go through probate court—things like a piece of property, your home perhaps which you own jointly with your wife; i.e., property which passes by "operation of law." Or a life insurance policy in which she is named the beneficiary. Or the benefits from a qualified profit-sharing plan at your company that go to her.

A will governs the distribution of probate assets, and without one that disposition of assets can be a long and costly process. It'll also entail the expenses of a court-appointed administrator.

A will allows you to name an executor, a person who administers the estate and carries out your expressed wishes.

Answer the Tough Nontax Questions

A will can also deal with any number of nontax questions that most people seldom even think about. What happens, Zobel asked, if you and your wife die in the same accident? You have two children, he reminded Slater. What about them?

When a husband and wife die simultaneously, there is a legal presumption about who dies first. It varies from state to state, and whatever your state presumes prevails. Arbitrarily, that could make a great difference to your estate and its taxes, but if you have a will you can rebut the legal presumption of the state. You can determine who for legal purposes dies first.

Drawing a will forces you to think about such a catastrophe, to decide whom you'd want to be guardian for the children and make arrangements with that person or persons. You can also put in the will what sort of discretion you want to give that person over the money you leave the children. Maybe your good friends who agree to take care of your children have to add a room to their house or buy a bigger house to bring your children into their family comfortably. Your will can allow them to draw funds from your estate to do that.

Such matters have nothing to do with taxes, Zobel told Slater, but they are profoundly important and are left unanswered without a will.

Slater agreed and said he would see his lawyer and have the document drawn. For the moment, he wanted to go back to a point Zobel had raised earlier concerning the marital deduction.

Protecting Your Spouse's Estate Too

Whatever you leave to your surviving spouse is tax-free to her, Zobel told him. That's the unlimited marital deduction. You don't get it, by the way, if you merely live together, unless you reside in a state that recognizes common law marriages. But otherwise everything from husband to wife or wife to husband is completely tax-free.

That he understood, but Zobel's earlier implication was that somehow even with a completely tax-free transfer of his entire estate he still had tax problems.

He wouldn't, or more accurately his estate would not, Zobel explained. The problem comes when his wife dies. Her estate, enlarged by what he had left her tax-free, might then face heavy taxes.

Slater wanted to know, quite naturally, if it was possible to avoid those taxes as well. It was a question most of

Zobel's clients reached at one point or another, and he had a standard whimsical answer for them.

"That's a cinch," he said, smiling.

Slater sat forward. "A cinch?"

First you leave everything to your wife, he told him. The marital deduction covers that. Then she leaves everything to charity. No taxes for anyone. A cinch.

Slater thought that was a wonderful plan, assuming they didn't care about their children.

Unfortunately, that was the larger point, Zobel observed. Life is trade-offs, and so is death. What it comes down to is that if your estate amounts to more than $1,200,000, you are probably going to face some estate taxes somewhere along the way.

That, Zobel explained, was the amount covered by the unified transfer tax credit for Slater and his wife. Each of them was entitled to a credit of $192,800, which would cover the taxes on $600,000. That meant Slater and his wife each could transfer assets up to that amount to somebody other than each other without any taxes.

So his estate could transfer to each of his two children, say, $300,000, and it would all be tax-free. (There are no federal inheritance taxes. Most states have them, but they tend to be a fairly low percentage of the amount of the inheritance.) Same for his wife and her estate. With planning, that would mean a total transfer of $1,200,000 without taxes.

The transfers may be made by the estates. Or they may be effected during their lifetimes, drawing on the same unified credit, unified in the sense that the credit covers both bequests from estates and gifts during a lifetime.

A $10,000 Gift, Tax-Free

In addition and quite apart from the unified credit is the annual gift tax exclusion. That entitles Slater and his wife each year to make gifts up to $10,000 ($20,000 jointly) to each child, or to any other person, relative or otherwise, and there is no tax on the gift. It can be a useful tool for shifting income within the family (see Chapters 6 and 7) and a way to move assets out of an estate with no tax consequences.

If Slater or his wife makes a gift that exceeds the $10,000–20,000 limit of the annual gift exclusion, the excess will be subject to gift taxes. However, they may be eliminated by applying a sufficient amount of the unified credit. Whatever is used during a lifetime means that much less to be applied against transfers from estates later on.

Slater was heartened, mainly because he thought he and his wife would pass easily under the $1,200,000 figure, and they were never going to be able to give their children more than $20,000 a year unless they won the state lottery. He'd be delighted to have the estate problems of a multimillionaire, but he'd be very surprised if he would end up leaving even $1.2 million.

Zobel thought he might have a surprise, a happy surprise, for Slater.

First, some questions to flesh out Slater's profile: What did he earn? What pension and profit-sharing plans did he participate in? The stocks, bonds, other assets he presently owned? The value of his home? Roughly what his living costs amounted to? Was he due to inherit anything substantial? The ages of his two children? How much insurance was he carrying? What sort of debts?

He also asked him questions that were intended to force

Slater to think: Where did he expect to be professionally in five years? If he died, how would his family's standard of living be affected? Presumably, from what Slater had already said, he wanted to care for his wife, then his children. Was his wife capable of administering an estate? Could she handle money?

That was not a sexist question, Zobel told him, but a realistic one. Many women, like many men, have trouble managing money. For the sake of any estate, it was important that a cool appraisal be rendered. If Slater's wife could manage the estate, fine. If not, who should be the administrator?

Not everything would be resolved in one session, Zobel told him, and gave him a booklet with additional questions for Slater to consider. "Do you feel each of your children should be treated equally re your estate distribution? Should your children receive their inheritance outright when they attain legal age if you and your spouse have died prior thereto? If not, at what age?"

The Toughest Question: What Do You Want?

Estate planning for Zobel is a matter of getting from point A to point B. A is where a client and his potential estate are at the moment. B is the point at which the estate is distributed after the client's death.

What's tough is defining point B, not getting there. What's tough is for the client to think through, with Zobel's guidance, what he wants to see happen.

Once that's done, the plan is implemented. Documents are written, and they can say anything the client wants.

As Zobel told Slater, an estate plan is entirely flexible. It's a living, breathing document and can do anything you want.

Similarly, a will is a flexible instrument, and it can include provisions to dispose of assets in any way you can imagine. It can assure you that your wishes will be carried out exactly.

One of Zobel's clients, for example, loved his son, but he always felt the young man was dull, stodgy. Worked well in the family business, but the father, who had a great zest for life, could never stir his son. "He is only 32 years old," the man told Zobel. "But you'd think he was 72. His idea of a hot Saturday night is a game of Trivial Pursuit. When I die, I wish he'd use some of the money I'm going to leave him to get a little excitement out of life. I mean, I'd like him to take a bundle of it and go buy himself a fire-engine-red Ferrari. Seriously, if I could, I'd write my will so he'd be forced to do that."

Zobel told him he could do exactly that, if he wanted. And he did. Right there in the will it says that "upon my death the executor is hereby instructed to purchase for my son Daniel a red Ferrari. If my son refuses to accept his gift, he is hereby excluded from every other provision for him in this document."

Keep Your Eye on the Middle Polaroid

As Zobel scratched notes and numbers on his pad, the raw data of Slater's financial life, he was juggling in his head. The estate planner is part juggler.

He is looking at the pieces that are in Slater's estate now. He is calculating what might be moved out before his death. He is imagining what will be left in the estate after his death.

As he explained it to Slater, try to imagine that we're taking three Polaroid pictures. One is taken of the estate a moment before death. One at the moment of death. One at the moment after death. What we have to focus on, so far as estate taxes are concerned, is the middle picture. What is in there at the moment of death?

That is what those awful taxes will be levied on. What's in that middle picture will be your gross estate. And the tax law is amazingly clear about what is includable and excludable in your gross estate. Section 2031 of the Internal Revenue Code says: "The value of the gross estate of the decedent shall be determined by including the value at the time of his death of all property, real or personal, tangible or intangible, wherever situated."

It is quite unambiguous. Whatever you own, to whatever extent that you own it, at the time of your death. Wherever located. So, you own a piece of property in England. Do you have to include it? Or Bermuda, a tax haven? The IRS doesn't want to hear about it. *Wherever situated* covers the universe.

The trick, Zobel explained, is to have as much in the first picture as we can and as little in the middle picture as we can.

And that means starting this very minute. Nothing personal, he told Slater, but he does estate planning on the theory that his client will die tomorrow.

How Much Is $1.2 Million?

He returned to his notes and told Slater that, as he suspected, Slater was in for a surprise. Most of his clients shared the experience. He was about to show Slater that $1,200,000 was not such an awful lot of money after all.

Slater was 48; his wife, 40. He is the only earner in the family, currently drawing $125,000 a year, which is about what he's been making for the last three years. He expects to work another 10 to 15 years, earning at the same and increasingly higher levels.

His home, which he bought 10 years ago for $75,000, is worth $250,000 today, mortgaged for $40,000.

Pension and profit-sharing plans are running about $350,000. For life insurance, he's carrying $100,000 on his own, with $250,000 more in group term provided by the company.

Plus, he's got his best earning years ahead of him. In the stretch between the time his last child finishes college and the time he retires, Slater will probably be able to save and invest $40,000–50,000 a year, which means another $600,000 in the estate.

Put it all together, Zobel said, and they were looking at a potential estate of $1,550,000, without taking into account any appreciation on the house or other investments, inheritances he or his wife might receive, any stock or stock options from his company.

Suddenly, the magic number of $1.2 million does not seem so magical.

Slater's situation and scenario is one Zobel encounters over and over again these days. Between a client's simple facts and inflation, it's not hard to end up with an estate of more than $1,200,000. Which only increases the need for planning.

Estate Taxes: Graduated and Staggering

Slater, however, was astonished. His first question now that Zobel had made him a millionaire was whether he or his wife would have to pay 50% of the $350,000 that was excess over $1,200,000 as estate taxes.

Zobel quickly assured him that they would not. It's a

graduated tax. The estate taxes would depend on the size of the estate.

On the numbers they just ran up, if one of you had the full $350,000 over and above your other assets—an estate worth $1,550,000—the estate tax on the $350,000 would be, according to the IRS table, $150,500. But if the $350,000 were sitting on top of an exclusion equivalent of $600,000 —an estate worth $950,000—then the tax on the same $350,000 would be less, $133,500.

That was still a staggering amount of money, Slater thought.

Zobel agreed, but those estate taxes could be avoided altogether.

Slater told him to keep talking.

Zobel suggested they take a close look at those trusts Slater had said he didn't like. They could save him the entire $150,500 in estate taxes.

An ILIT to the Rescue

As Zobel explained, for a situation like Slater's there were two kinds of trusts he might most likely recommend. One was an irrevocable life insurance trust (an ILIT or Crummey trust, named after the taxpayer who litigated the leading case involving ILITs; the other was a bypass trust).

They could create an ILIT to own and be the beneficiary of all the insurance policies. So when Slater dies, all the proceeds of the insurance policies, which presently amount to $350,000, would be removed from his estate and pass to the insurance trust. That would remove the taxable excess from his estate, and everything else—$1.2 million—would go to his wife, all covered by the marital deduction.

The $350,000 in the ILIT would be invested by Slater's trustee, and Slater's trust could stipulate that all of the income from the trust should go to his wife during her lifetime.

Further, he might add something called a *five or five power*, which would allow his wife to withdraw each year from the capital of the trust 5% of the trust or $5000, whichever is greater.

When she dies, that $350,000 trust is not in her estate, so her estate pays no taxes on it. By making his wife only a life income beneficiary—she does not have control of the $350,000 itself—he excludes the trust assets from her middle Polaroid. And by another provision they would put in Slater's trust, the whole trust could pass at that time to his children, and the whole amount would be free of estate taxes to either Slater's or his wife's estate.

In other words, by creating and using the ILIT, Slater will have saved his wife's estate the $150,500 in estate taxes it might otherwise have had to pay; he will have provided considerable income to his wife during her lifetime; and he will have provided a substantial tax-free bundle for each of his children after his wife dies.

And, Zobel added, to deal with a concern Slater raised early in their session, an ILIT should cost about $1000 to set up, maybe $300 a year to administer. Not too onerous on a saving of more than $150,000 in estate tax.

How Much Insurance?

It all sounded very good to Slater. He only wondered if he should be thinking about buying more life insurance. It was hard to know what to believe when it comes to life insurance.

Zobel told him that for estate planning insurance has three purposes.

First, some people need it to create an estate. Otherwise

they wouldn't be leaving their spouse and family with anything. Obviously, those are people who don't have much in the way of other assets. Obviously, that is not Slater.

Other people buy insurance to cover specific estate needs, say, to pay the estate taxes. Or, to be sure that educational costs are covered, insurance might be stuck into an education trust. With two children yet to go through college, that might be something to consider for Slater.

Insurance is also used to replace income. In a family where the man is the only or certainly larger earner, and where his death would greatly cut the family's cash flow, insurance is bought to compensate and allow the family to maintain its normal standard of living.

In Slater's case, if he were to die tomorrow, that could be a problem for his wife and children. Looking further ahead, toward the years when his children have finished college and presumably are on their own, conditions will be quite different.

The solution, Zobel suggested, might be additional term insurance, which he might be able to buy as an extension of the coverage he now has through his company. That could cover him for the immediate years and then be dropped when it was no longer really needed.

Bypass Trust and AB Trust Will

Getting back to the will itself and Slater's general planning, Zobel said that another mechanism they should consider was the bypass trust.

Basically, the bypass would allow Slater to shift assets from his estate to the trust and then to his children, bypassing estate taxes to his wife's estate. In a common formula, if the estate is large enough, he would leave the first $600,000 —his unified credit exemption equivalent—to the trust and everything else to his wife. The trust income would go to his wife, the remainder to his children on her death.

This is a widely used approach, Zobel told him. You could go to any lawyer and say, "I want an AB trust will," and he knows just what to draw up for you, a marital deduction A trust and a bypass B trust. It's all there in 10 or 11 pages.

Quite simple. But worth a lot of money. The bypass trust that would remove $600,000 from his wife's estate could save them $235,000 in aggregate estate taxes.

Slater rather liked the AB trust approach. One size fits all, almost.

Zobel shrugged. His was a more complex view. Many people, he said, don't want to take that approach for a variety of reasons. One client with an estate of close to $4 million wants to leave everything to his wife, not a single trust in the plan, so that she can have complete and unrestricted control of all the assets.

He is confident not only that she will manage the $4 million during her lifetime but that she will also do estate planning, to arrange for shares of the family fortune to pass to their children and to minimize her own estate taxes.

A Last Resort: The Disclaimer

Whether he wants it or not, the man's surviving wife will have the right to "disclaim" a portion of the estate when he dies.

If she decides at that time that even though his intention was loving it might not be the wisest course from a tax perspective, she could disclaim a portion of the estate. And that portion would be treated as if she had died first. It might go to their children, or if his will provided for one, it could go into a trust.

The "disclaimer" is something of a last chance the law gives everyone to correct any error that might have been made in a will or overlooked in planning the estate.

Do Not Cast Your Will in Stone

Toward the end of their session, Slater returned to the AB will as something that would suit his needs.

Zobel suggested Slater and his attorney draw a will on that basis now and that he, Zobel, should be part of the meeting. But they should also bear in mind that life changes.

Wills should be reviewed every two or three years or whenever there's a significant change in life, Zobel told him. The normal process allows you to make ongoing adjustments. Perhaps you decide the gift you were going to leave your college isn't enough. Perhaps your daughter has graduated from business school and married the heir to one of America's great fortunes, while your son has had yet another business failure. Adjustments to deal with any such matters can be handled easily with a will review and change.

Some people draw a will, put it in a safe deposit box (which can make it very difficult to get ahold of at the time of death), and forget about it for years and years.

Zobel told Slater one horror story of a daughter who showed up with such a will left by her mother. The woman and her husband had made the will years ago, typically drawn it so everything went to each other, the surviving spouse. But no thought had been given in the intervening years to new laws or to planning as the value of the estate appreciated.

The result was that the woman left an estate in excess of

her $600,000 exclusion by some $250,000. It meant the estate would have to pay taxes of more than $94,000.

If they had done any updating, Zobel observed, they could have used any of the trusts we discussed or other instruments and completely avoided $94,000 in estate taxes.

Or maybe on a review you see that the size of your estate is beginning to increase and your personal cash flow is improving to the point where you should and can take advantage of the $10,000 annual gift exclusion mentioned earlier.

Maybe you put a plan into effect where you and your wife start making gifts of $20,000 a year to your son and the same amount to your daughter. That can add up, in terms of both what you are passing along to your children and what you are removing tax-free from your estate. In five years you've shifted $200,000. As Senator Dirksen used to say, a billion here, a billion there, and pretty soon we're talking about real money.

Or perhaps you finally hit a bonanza. Your company has been sold, accepts a friendly offer. With all the stock you hold in the company by that time, your net worth increases by $10 million. Time to reshape your will and replan your ominously large estate.

Slater enjoyed that one. At $10 million, he reflected, he would have terrible estate tax problems. Could Zobel do all his juggling, spin out a bypass here, an ILIT there, and get them home tax-free?

On $10 million, Zobel allowed, it was not so easy. It certainly has been tried. What you can do, how much you can do, depends on a lot of factors. But the truth is, it's not so easy.

They agreed that it would be nice, however, if they did have such problems to wrestle with.

Checklist: Chapter 8

Tax-smart strategies and perspectives for you to consider and discuss with your tax professional:

1. Bear in mind that estate taxes can run as high as 50%, more than you pay on ordinary income. The high stakes make estate planning critical. Even with relatively modest estates, taxes can easily run into the tens of thousands of dollars.

2. Have a will and keep it current. Review it every two or three years or whenever there's a significant change in life.

Without a will, the state will intervene and according to its law divide your estate, giving portions to people you may not want to help at all.

If the will is not current, the estate could end up being divided in ways that no longer represent your wishes. And, if out of date and not consistent with current law, it could result in estate taxes that otherwise might have been avoided.

3. A will also forces you to cope with nontax questions; e.g., in the event you and your spouse are killed in an accident, who is to be the guardian of your children and what provisions the estate is to make to pay for the guardian's additional living expenses brought on by your children.

4. The unlimited marital deduction allows one spouse to pass to the other his or her entire estate with absolutely no estate or other taxes on it, no matter how large the estate might be or in what form its assets are.

Normally this deduction is a central part of any estate plan and, as noted, allows a completely tax-free transfer. However, the plan then must consider what can be done to avoid or minimize estate taxes when the surviving spouse dies and his or her estate then includes all of those assets that were passed on to him or her.

5. The unified transfer tax credit gives every taxpayer a credit of $192,800 that covers the estate and/or gift taxes on $600,000.

The credit may be applied during a lifetime for gifts or at death against transfers from an estate to any individual (other than spouse, of course, who is covered by the unlimited marital deduction).

This means that a married couple may jointly transfer $1,200,000 to others without taxes.

6. The $10,000 annual gift exclusion allows each taxpayer to make gifts of $10,000 a year, or $20,000 if the gift is from a couple, without any gift taxes.

Over those amounts, there might be gift taxes, but the unified credit may be applied to eliminate the taxes. Whatever is used of the credit during a lifetime is deducted from the total credit and leaves that much less to be applied against transfers from estates later on.

7. To produce an estate plan, you should provide your planner with basic financial data—your present assets? value of your home? current and projected earnings? amount of insurance being carried?—as well as answers to questions related to the future such as, if you died, how would your family's standard of living be affected, and is your spouse capable of managing money and handling your estate?

8. Estate planning basically consists of getting from point A to point B, from the point where you and your estate are now to the point when your estate will be distributed after you die. The tough part is figuring out what you really want to happen at point B.

9. Bear in mind that a will can be completely flexible, providing for the disposition of assets in any way you desire.

And a trust is the perfect flexible legal instrument to complement the will. Contrary to popular opinion, trusts need not be expensive to create or maintain.

10. Consider setting up an irrevocable life insurance trust (ILIT) that can be the beneficiary of your life insurance. That would remove it from your estate, yet the income from the trust may go to your surviving spouse during his or her lifetime, with the remainder of the trust passing tax-free to your children on your spouse's death.

11. A bypass trust is another broader use of the trust form. Typically assets up to $600,000, the amount covered by the unified credit, are passed to the bypass trust, which removes them from the decedent's estate and bypasses the surviving spouse and her subsequent estate.

As with the ILIT, the income may go to the surviving spouse, and on his or her death the trust is distributed tax-free to the heirs.

12. An AB trust will is the common form of a will that includes a marital deduction A trust and a bypass B trust. It is a widely used plan that serves a vast number of estates.

13. The law allows a surviving spouse the right to disclaim any assets willed to him or her. They are then passed to a trust and like the above kept out of the surviving spouse's estate.

This device is a kind of last chance permitted by the law that allows anyone to correct errors that might have been made in a will or overlooked in planning the estate.

9
Estate Planning:
Heavy Hitters

Estate planning is an engaging intellectual pursuit. Spanning complicated sections of the tax code, requiring the application and tailoring of various legal instruments and strategies by CPAs and lawyers, it can mean the difference between keeping hundreds of thousands of dollars within your family and having it dissolve into taxes.

Jeffrey Slater in the previous chapter was fairly typical of Robert Zobel's clients. He started out with no knowledge and relatively simple problems and became in one meeting intrigued with the possibility of getting on top of the law, as he put it. In no time he was captured by the vision of paying no estate taxes on an estate of $10 million.

Was that possible? he wanted to know. To create a plan so deftly that it averted some $5 million in estate taxes on an estate with 10 million taxable dollars?

Unlikely, Zobel had told him.

A few weeks later John McNally was asking Zobel essentially the same questions, but not out of intellectual curiosity. He was sitting on an estate that somewhat exceeded $10 million, he had suffered one major heart attack only a year earlier, and he wanted desperately to avoid anything like $5 million in estate taxes.

He was a builder who had also invested well in Florida real estate. He had moved to Florida from Pennsylvania in the late 1950s, when it appeared that half of America was moving there to do something or other connected with missiles. In those days it was hard to lose money building homes and offices. McNally also did very well developing a couple of shopping centers.

Most of his work was along Florida's east coast, and the decline of that real estate market in the 1970s is history. But by that time McNally had made his fortune, and being a fairly cautious man anyway, he avoided a number of investment traps and cut way back on his building operation.

That was just as well so far as his wife, Marge, and his doctor were concerned. McNally figured he must have had high blood pressure since he was four and been overweight since then as well. A classic candidate for a heart attack, he had conformed to type about a year before he went to Zobel.

If he had died then, at age 66, he did at least have a will, and everything would have passed to his wife. The unlimited marital deduction would cover that transfer and eliminate any estate taxes at that point at least. They had four children, and except for minimal and sentimental bequests —a ring, a watch, $10,000 to each child—nothing was directed to them.

There were no trusts set up. There was not even a plan that would take advantage of John's $600,000 exemption under the unified credit. That would evaporate on his death.

Transfer Assets While You Can

Before the meeting with McNally, Zobel had read his existing will and shaped ideas of how it might be altered. But even before discussing those, there was another strategy.

"We've got to lighten your load," Zobel told him. He explained that if McNally died tomorrow, everything could pass without taxes to his wife, but she would then be saddled with the same huge estate. To be sure, she was 10 years younger than he and in good health, which would give her time to diminish the size of the estate and its potential taxes.

But they shouldn't wait, he told McNally. He didn't want to alarm McNally, who insisted he was in better health than he ever had been, already 25 pounds lighter than he was a year ago when he had the heart attack. They had another urgent trimming process.

They had to transfer assets out of the estate.

That started with the simple $10,000 annual gift exclusion, $20,000 if he and his wife gave jointly. They should begin shifting chunks of $20,000 every year, he advised McNally. That's a freebie the law gives you. Take advantage of it.

If you envision your estate eventually being divided in one fashion or another among your four children, start making joint gifts to them of $20,000 a year. That's $80,000 a year.

The same holds for anyone else you would eventually want to help, possibly a brother, sister, another relative, a good friend. Start making gifts to them now.

Use the Unified Credit Before It Gets Cut

McNally should go beyond that, far beyond it, and use up the $600,000 unified credit exemption he and his wife are each entitled to now. Don't wait until one of you dies.

Make gifts to your children and anyone else you want and apply the unified credit.

Presently, the law says you may give away up to $600,000 each. But there's nothing that prevents Congress from changing the law, as it has before, Zobel warned him. The annual exclusion for gifts used to be only $3000, $30,000 in a lifetime. Take full advantage of what the law presently allows.

Further, if you make a gift of, say, $100,000 to one of your children, and that money gets invested, it could grow nicely over a period of years. Maybe in 10 years they've got not $100,000 but $500,000 in that pot.

That is half a million dollars your child is going to possess outright, which you have in a sense given him or her, but it is not going to be any part of your estate.

If you do that for each of the four children, that is $2 million dollars on which neither you nor your wife will have to worry about estate taxes.

Safeguard: Durable Power of Attorney

As they turned to consider McNally's existing will, Zobel told him he had some thoughts on how to update and change it, some tax-saving thoughts.

First, a suggestion that McNally might want to review with his attorney. Separate from the new will, they might create what is called a *durable power of attorney*, which would be granted to someone, normally whoever will be the trustee of the estate.

This will empower someone you trust to act on your behalf if you should fall ill and are incapable of acting. Zobel added that he didn't mean to scare McNally, but he had suffered one heart attack, and the provision was tailored for people with health questions.

It could make a meaningful difference to an estate, Zobel told him. One of his clients did not have such a power assigned and got cancer. His days were numbered, and though his family knew, they didn't want to tell him.

As the cancer spread, the poor man became semicomatose and incoherent most of the time. Yet there was no way anyone could act on his estate on his behalf. No one had the power to do so.

In that case, for example, if his executor had a durable power of attorney and saw the end coming quickly, he might have gone out and purchased "flower bonds," long-term Treasury bonds that are sold at significant discount. They pay a very low rate of return, 2–3%, but they have a unique quality: If they are held in the decedent's name at his death, they may be used to pay estate taxes, and they are redeemed at par.

It was clear that the estate was facing taxes of some $200,000. The year before, the man had set up an ILIT as the beneficiary of his life insurance. But the law says that if any such transfer of life insurance occurs within three years of death, the life insurance is taxable in the estate on death.

If someone had the durable power of attorney, he could have gone into the market and bought $200,000 worth of flower bonds for the estate. At the time they were selling down around 65 and at par of course were worth 100, a tremendous saving. Or it might have been for the estate.

But nothing could be done. The man died in a couple of months, and a special investment opportunity was lost.

So, Zobel concluded, not to be ghoulish, but that is well worth serious thought.

The Q-TIP Special

Out of their discussion it became clear to Zobel that McNally had a worry. He loved and trusted his wife, but he thought that $10 million was an awful lot of money. He wanted some plan that would at the same time provide for his wife and assure that his children would inherit the remainder of all those millions after she died. But, if it was possible, she should be allowed to determine exactly which child received how much, within limits.

As McNally wisely perceived, some years from now only she could decide which children had the greatest need for the money.

Zobel's solution was a Qualified Terminable Interest in Property or Q-TIP trust, which is a marital trust with special conditions. On McNally's instructions in his will, his executor would put all of his assets, say $10 million, into the Q-TIP trust. His wife would not receive any of the assets directly, but she would receive all of the income from the $10 million.

Furthermore, his will would give her a *special power of appointment*, the power to divide the trust on her death among the four children as she sees fit, within specified guidelines, say not less than 20% or more than 50% to any one child. And, if she did not divide it that way, it would get split equally among the four.

With a plan like that, Zobel told him, McNally could relax. His wife would certainly live well on the income of a $10 million Q-TIP trust, yet there was no question that his children would ultimately benefit, according to their needs as his wife saw it.

Estate Planning: Heavy Hitters

McNally was impressed, and he told Zobel that. He would be even more impressed if Zobel could also come up with a plan that would eliminate the estate taxes that would eventually be dumped on that Q-TIP when it came time to distribute the assets out of it.

Unfortunately, he had no magic that would make estate taxes vanish, Zobel told him. But all during his wife's remaining years they would do what they could to transfer assets from the trust to the children, using her annual $10,000 gift exclusion and any of her $600,000 unified credit umbrella, if any was left.

Expect the IRS at Your Grave

But in the end there would be a day of reckoning, probably with an IRS audit attached to it. The IRS audits a higher percentage of big estates than any other kind of return because their rewards for such audits can be so substantial. And also, of course, it's their last chance to collect from you.

That disturbed McNally almost as much as the estate tax bill itself. All his life, he told Zobel, he broke his back and paid his taxes, lots and lots of taxes. And then, as if that's not enough, they come around the other way when he's six feet under.

Zobel offered his sympathies. But where was it written that the tax law, new or old, had to be fair? The only time the word *fair* appears in the Internal Revenue Code, he told him, is in describing *fair market value*. If it was any consolation, McNally was not alone. Zobel had a client in the other day with an estate almost twice the size of McNally's, facing the same problems.

In that case, the man had two daughters. He wanted to make sure they shared in his estate, and he didn't think they should have to account to their mother for the money nor did he want them to wait until she died before they got it.

His idea was to leave each daughter $2.5 million after he died, free of any tax.

His problem was that if he did that, the federal estate tax would amount to some $4 million.

The reason it would be so high was that the balance of his estate was to go to his wife and qualify for the marital deduction but the tax free bequests to his daughters would reduce his wife's share of the estate and the funds to pay the estate taxes.

Unfortunately the amount used to pay the estate tax means that there must be an even greater taxable estate in order to pay those estate taxes, which means more comes from the wife's share, and on and on in a circular calculation that is done when an estate is divided and is also paying all related federal and state taxes.

The net effect would have been a federal estate tax almost as large as the bequest to the daughters. His wife would have ended up with $11 million, but the tax bill would have been staggering.

But as Zobel figured out, there was a way to slice those numbing taxes. If the man left the entire $20 million to his wife instead, with the understanding that she would divide $5 million between the girls, then instead of a $4 million estate tax, there would be only gift taxes of about $2,225,000. That would leave his wife with another $1,750,000 of the estate than otherwise, a total of about $12,750,000.

Reflecting on his own earlier concern, McNally wondered how the man could be certain the gifts would be made as he wanted if he didn't make the gifts in his lifetime. How could he be sure with Zobel's plan?

It was a good question. In fact, Zobel replied, he has to take a leap of faith and trust his wife to follow his wishes.

Why not protect the whole thing with a Q-TIP, McNally asked, as you did with me?

Because then his daughters would have to wait until his wife's death before they received any money. This way they would get it on his death, one way or the other.

McNally returned to the bottom line. Zobel's plan would save the family $1,750,000, which was sensational, and yet they still faced an unbelievable tax bill of $2,225,000. Were there no ways to get around such a terrible blow?

In that case there was nothing further Zobel could devise. To be sure, there are sometimes circumstances, he told McNally, where the nature of the assets is such that you can get a break.

The Asset Freeze: No Taxes on $8.5 Million . . .

Unfortunately, the cases where Zobel was able to deflect estate taxes did not apply to McNally. They concerned family businesses where assets could be frozen (a maneuver Zobel's colleague William Raby discusses in Chapter 5 with his client, George Udal, in connection with future possibilities for the closely held family corporation he was starting).

In one situation two brothers wanted to ensure that each side of the family would always own 50% of the company and at the same time to freeze the value of their assets in the company.

Zobel's plan was to recapitalize the company, each brother passing over his shares of common stock in the company and receiving shares of preferred stock, $100 par value, along with shares of new common stock.

The common was reshuffled among their children, each side of the family still owning 50%. The voting rights remained with the preferred stock while all of the appreciation in the company belongs to the common.

Everything was shifted around tax-free, the whole plan even blessed by a private letter ruling from the IRS.

That was in 1975. The company today is worth about $10 million. But only $750,000 of that will appear in each brother's estate. That's the value of his preferred stock.

Which means that $8.5 million belongs to the children and now grandchildren, as the stock has been passed down as gifts through the family.

There will not be a penny of estate tax on the $8.5 million when the brothers die. Eventually, when and if the children sell their stock, they will have to pay an income tax on the gain. But if that were to happen in 1988, it would be a maximum of 28–33%, rather than 50% that would have been exacted if it had been estate tax. And, of course, no law says they have to sell the stock now or for many years. It might be passed along to others in the family.

. . . Or, $5 Million

In another case Zobel created a new holding company for a family business as the tax-smart solution.

In that one, almost a dream situation, a client bought about 90% of a company that was about to disappear, for all of $12,000.

He began to revive this particular company and along the way to buy up the stock he didn't own.

In the process of buying that stock, a clear valuation was fixed on the stock, an aspect of this maneuver the IRS looks at closely.

Once again the plan called for the client to exchange his common stock for preferred, which was valued at $200,000.

His wife was given $100,000 of preferred. Their children received 1000 shares of common, which they bought for cash.

Then the whole company was merged into a new family holding company.

The father died about two years ago. The value of that stock in his estate was still only $200,000. The company bought back the wife's preferred for $100,000, on which she had to pay a capital gains tax of 20%.

The children presently own 100% of the stock of the company, and it is worth some $5 million.

There has been no estate tax, gift tax, and essentially no income tax on any of it.

It was a story McNally relished, a piece of planning he labeled "beautiful." If only Zobel could do the same for him. No estate tax, no gift tax, no income tax.

"If only I could," Zobel said to him. On the other hand, they hadn't done too badly. In one session they had saved hundreds of thousands of dollars in estate taxes. Not a bad day's work, they agreed.

Checklist: Chapter 9

Tax-smart strategies and perspectives for you to consider and discuss with your tax professional:

1. With large estates, start unloading. Transfer assets out of the estate during your lifetime.

Use the $10,000 annual gift exclusion, $20,000 jointly, to make regular gifts in those amounts to children and all other people you would otherwise be including in your will.

Make use of the unified credit during your lifetime. Go beyond the annual gift exclusion and give up to $600,000. That is the maximum presently covered by the credit, but the law has changed over the years and might change again. Take advantage of what the law allows now.

Such a plan shifts $600,000 from your estate and spares the estate those potential taxes. Further, if a gift is made now and invested, it could multiply many times, which would increase the value of your gift many times. However, the appreciation will all be outside your estate and so without any estate tax consequences.

2. Consider a durable power of attorney. It provides someone you trust with the legal power to act on behalf of your estate, should you fall ill and be incapable of doing so. This is especially recommended for people with any questionable medical history.

3. A qualified terminable interest in property, a Q-TIP trust, is a marital trust with special conditions. It enables you to have assets from your estate placed in a trust to designate who will be the recipient of income from the trust and how the remainder of the trust will be distributed on that recipient's death.

4. A special power of appointment, used together with the Q-TIP, assigns the right to a survivor to determine how the trust's assets will be divided on her or his death, within more general guidelines established by the original will.

5. Where the primary assets in an estate are stock in a closely held family corporation, those assets might be frozen by using preferred stock for the parents, common stock going to the children. All of the appreciated value in the company and the stock is reflected in the value of the common, while the preferred remains frozen. The only value, then, reflected in the estate of the parent is that of the preferred. All of the appreciated value passes to the children outside of the parent's estate and thus is free of any estate taxes.

10
Retirement Plans: The Tax Law Still Has a Heart, Sort Of

Retirement planning is a tough area for most people, and the Tax Reform Act did not make it any easier.

To begin with, there is the perfectly normal, pervasive anxiety that most of us have about the future. We want to be assured that we will be able to live comfortably, not to say in the style to which we've become accustomed, 10 years from now, 20 or more years from now. And we want that assurance, even though the rational side of us says, Who can be certain of anything so far in the future?

Not only do we want certainty; we want clarity. We want formulas. We want a plan that will guide us from now to then.

The truth is there are no simple plans. There are, to be sure, critical questions to be considered.

When do you expect to retire? How many years does that leave you to prepare economically?

How much do you think you're going to need to live on then, factoring in the likely amount of inflation over the years as well as a new lifestyle?

Where is that money going to come from?

There are in other words ways of estimating, and there are strategies that should help you reach a level of some economic security when you arrive at that distant land of retirement. But there is no magical formula, and there is no certainty.

The tax laws figure heavily in all this, as we'll see, encouraging retirement saving, giving you and your employer deductions for retirement plan contributions, allowing you to compound investments made through retirement plans tax-free.

But there is a simpler element in the equation that is also of enormous importance, and it is systematic accumulation.

In a way, one of the great benefits of the various retirement plans has nothing to do with taxes: the plans practically force you to save for retirement. Indeed, if you had no retirement plan and instead had the willpower to systematically put some 6% of your income into a money market fund, a mutual fund, or a stock with reasonable selectivity and luck, from the day you began to work, you would end up just as well off or better when you reached retirement age.

Deductions and Other Benefits

As a matter of policy, the federal government recognizes the need and importance of retirement planning by indirectly subsidizing your plans.

With "qualified" plans—ones that meet the many requirements of the tax law, most of which are intended to protect employees—companies are allowed to deduct the contribution to the retirement plan and you do not have to pay taxes on that contribution. That's one form of subsidy.

Furthermore, as the funds in your plan are invested and

earn for you, those earnings are not taxed year by year. The earnings are allowed to increase and compound on a tax-deferred basis, and only when you draw out the funds are they and you taxed. And even then there are possible tax breaks.

With the Tax Reform Act, Congress got less generous and cut back on some of its subsidies.

The IRA Cuts

The change that got the most media attention concerned the IRA, though it was not by any means the most radical change of the many wrought by the new law on retirement programs.

The IRA had been available to everyone. You could contribute up to $2000 a year, $2250 if the plan was to cover both you and a nonworking spouse, and the nicest part of all, deduct the whole amount.

No taxes on the earnings until you drew it out, then taxed as ordinary income, which is the way your salary is taxed.

Now under the Tax Reform Act those rules obtain only if neither you nor your spouse is covered by any qualified retirement plan at work.

If either of you is covered, then you have a chance at the old benefits only if your joint adjusted gross income is below $40,000, or below $25,000 for unmarried individuals.

Between $40,000 and $50,000, or between $25,000 and $35,000, the deduction of the contribution is phased out.

You may still contribute up to $2000 or $2250 to an IRA, but you get no deduction on it.

The tax-deferred benefit on the fund and its earnings is also still allowed.

With your 1987 return, you face the choice for the first

time. Should you make the IRA contribution even though you no longer get the deduction, since the fund may still grow tax-deferred, or put the same amount into something like a tax-free bond? (See Chapters 1 and 2.)

If you do make the contribution, keep track of it and any other nondeductible contributions you make to your IRA in future years. When it comes time to draw the money out, the nondeductible portion will be tax-free.

Hitting Big Earners: 401(k) Plans

Generally, with the TRA, Congress was in a mood to curb the retirement and profit-sharing benefits of the biggest earners. Some of its measures dwarfed the IRA limitations.

For example, 401(k) plans.

These are popular qualified retirement plans that allowed an employee to take up to 15% of his income or $30,000, whichever was less, and put it into the retirement fund.

The law said that since the employee did not "constructively" receive that income the year it went into the 401(k), he would not have to pay any taxes on it.

That translated into a fairly sizable amount of money that you would not have any taxes on for the year of the contribution. And, if you could afford to put away $20,000 or $30,000 a year, which would grow tax-deferred, you would soon have a truly substantial fund.

Congress decided those funds were too substantial. With the TRA, it lowered the amount of the employee contribution to $7000.

If the company wants to make an additional contribution to the employee's 401(k), subject to antidiscrimination rules, it may add up to $23,000 or bring the total back to $30,000.

But it would require a most generous company to do so, and even if some contribution were added, there would be no additional deduction from income by the employee.

While the new ceiling is painful for many who participate in 401(k) plans, there is little doubt about their continuing value. In fact, perhaps they are more valuable now than ever. With the sweeping elimination by the Tax Reform Act of so many previous techniques to shelter income, the 401(k) and indeed other qualified retirement plans become one of the few remaining places where you may put your money, deduct it from your taxable income, and enjoy tax-deferred investing.

Other rules were written into the new law for 401(k) plans, especially antidiscrimination rules. These are written into all qualified retirement and profit-sharing plans to prevent an individual or a handful of individuals at the top of a company from providing benefits for themselves that they don't in some proportionate way provide for other employees who meet the qualifications for participation in the company's plan or plans.

These new 401(k) antidiscrimination rules as well as those like them added to other plans were another part of the congressional effort to curb big earners.

Check Your Defined Benefit Plan

This is especially apparent in the changes on qualified defined benefit plans.

These are extremely attractive plans that provide you with a specified or defined benefit in your retirement on a monthly or an annual basis for as long as you live. The amount is determined by a formula connected to your compensation from the company.

You might, for example, receive payments equal to 60%

of your average annual earnings over your last five years with the company.

Or it might be 1% of your annual compensation for the last five years, times the number of years you have been working for the company. So, if you have been there 25 years, you are entitled to 25% of your average compensation for the last five years. If that turns out to be an average of $100,000 a year, you would get $25,000 a year for life.

Your employer funds the plan according to the calculations of an actuary. He takes your data along with those of all the other employees who are qualified for the plan and factors in a number of elements, e.g., life expectancies, expected turnover, anticipated increases in compensation, as well as the projected return on the fund's investments.

Then he tells the employer, okay, for this year you should contribute $173,000 to the fund. In theory, if the actuary is reasonably accurate in his projections, and the employer makes the recommended contributions, there will be sufficient funds to provide you with the defined benefits you expect after you retire.

Obviously, a plan like this could provide a most substantial benefit to highly compensated employees. Under the old law there was a ceiling of $90,000. That was the maximum annual benefit you could receive, and you could start drawing it at age 62.

If you retired earlier, the amount of the benefit was to be scaled down actuarily since you'd be receiving the benefit that much longer. However, if you retired at 55 or later, the benefit could not drop below $75,000.

The Tax Reform Act drastically changes this, and the results could be catastrophic.

The $90,000 ceiling remains, but that full benefit does not begin until age 65. Now, if you retire at age 62, with a typical plan you would receive only $72,000, quite a drop from the previous $90,000.

Worse news for early retirees. If the company pushes you out the door at age 55, as an increasing number are doing these days, instead of the $75,000 minimum, you might now receive only $37,000. If it's age 60, only $59,000.

There is an important exception. If your plan had been in existence by May 6, 1986, and your accrued benefits already exceeded the new limits, you may still operate under the old rules for the amount that had accrued by that date.

But otherwise, if you had been counting on a defined benefit plan as an important part of your whole retirement program, review it carefully with your retirement adviser. There could be much less there than you thought, thanks to tax reform.

Warning: New 15% Tax

Another strike against big earners is the new excise tax on what Congress considers excessive distributions from retirement plans.

You might still be entitled to $90,000 from your defined benefit plan, for example, and in addition, from your IRA, from a profit-sharing plan, from a Keogh you funded in connection with free-lance consulting work, you are looking forward to another $50,000 a year in retirement benefit payouts.

That's too much, the new law contends.

Anything over $112,500 in yearly distributions from all qualified plans is now ruled excessive. And on the amount over $112,500, which for you would be $27,500, you will be taxed at a flat 15%, or $4125.

If you take the benefits in a lump-sum distribution rather than annual payments, the new ceiling from all your plans is $562,000. Over that amount, and you pay the 15% tax on the excess.

You can somewhat avoid these limits if your qualified benefits accrued before August 1, 1986, and the total of them at that time was greater than $562,500. Under those circumstances your distributions will be figured on a pro rata basis, to screen the pre–August 1, 1986, amounts from the 15% tax.

While the new limits, $112,500 and $562,500, are meaningful amounts, they are not by any means excessive for any executive of a large corporation, owner of a successful small business, lawyer, doctor, or any number of professionals, and apparently anybody who works on Wall Street.

For all of those big earners, replanning of existing retirement plans and their distributions is mandatory, or tens of thousands of dollars from those retirement benefits could end up being used to cover that 15% tax.

Congress Becomes Half as Humane

The change on 10-year forward averaging will affect not only top earners.

Ten-year forward averaging was a humane provision. It anticipated what could be a potentially horrible surprise when it finally came time to receive all that nice retirement money that had been growing for years and years.

While the money that your employer and perhaps you as well had contributed to the qualified plan was being invested and hopefully earning for you, all its earnings were tax-deferred, allowed to grow without any taxes until you drew them out. And then there would be the day of reckoning.

If this happy process of annual growth and appreciation goes on for many years, the amount you finally draw out of the fund could easily be in the middle six figures for a middle-level executive, seven figures for a top executive.

With most qualified plans, the distributions were taxed as ordinary income, your highest rate. If in the year of retirement you took a lump sum out of the fund in full settlement of your rights, it was as if you suddenly received a gigantic bonus. At ordinary income rates you were facing the possibility of giving 50% of it to the government, an event that could wreck the way you planned to live in retirement.

The tax law had a heart. Ten-year forward averaging allowed you to figure the tax as if you were being paid the retirement benefit over a 10-year period. Obviously, spread out as if it were in 10 installments, your tax should be greatly reduced.

You paid according to the tax schedule for a single person filing with that amount of income, multiplied by 10 for the 10 years. On that basis you could be spared a lot of taxes and grief.

Congress has become half as generous and humane. Ten-year averaging has been cut to five-year averaging.

If you reached age 50 by January 1, 1986, you may still elect 10-year and base your tax on 1986 rates. Or take five-year based on the existing tax rates for the year of your distribution.

The Rollover Maneuver

How you handle the big payout depends on a number of factors in your life.

You might not need all that money at that time. Perhaps you have a plan to become a consultant in your field, and maybe your former company is going to be one of your clients. (Though if that is your plan, be very certain that you have separated from service with that company and are no longer an employee, or you are going to invite trouble from the IRS over the legitimacy of your retirement fund payout. They will claim that you are still an employee of the old place, not an independent contractor, and that you are therefore not entitled to the retirement fund distribution. Early withdrawal of those funds could mean a penalty of 10% on the amount paid out to you.)

In addition to the income you expect from your new consulting business, you figure you'll need less to live on. Your children are grown, through college, and on their own. Your daily expenses are going to be less. And even though, as noted in Chapter 1, the new law is tougher on offices in homes, you are definitely going to qualify for one of those, which will save you tax dollars.

With that perspective you might choose a rollover. Take your lump-sum distribution from the company and roll it over into an IRA. If you are younger than 70½, the age when the law requires you to start drawing out of an IRA, you may roll over the retirement fund and not be taxed on any of it until you take it out. Over 70½, and you may roll it over into an IRA, but you would still be required to distribute from that IRA, so your advantage would be diminished.

Otherwise, rolled over, your distribution will continue to enjoy that wonderful tax-deferred status, which might well be the best thing that could happen to your fund.

Applying the rollover strategy might also spare you the new 15% excise tax. Perhaps your lump-sum payout exceeds $562,500, the new limit, and you would be faced with the 15% excise tax on the excess over that ceiling.

If you roll it over into an IRA, there would be no tax on any of it now. When you finally do draw it out of the IRA, it could be in annual installments below $112,500, so you could avoid the new tax altogether.

There is one trade-off with this strategy: When you reach 70½, and you must begin to draw funds out of the

IRA, if you want to take the money in a lump sum you will not be able to elect either 10-year or five-year forward averaging. Under old law and new, they are not allowed for IRA distributions, which are taxed as ordinary income.

Even so, the rollover and the additional years of tax-deferred growth of your fund might be worth the trade-off.

The same rollover technique may used if you are switching jobs and expect to continue working for a number of years. Once again you find yourself in a situation where you don't need or want the retirement fund that has accumulated in your first employer's plan. You simply roll it over into your new employer's plan, within 60 days of receiving it.

Beware: Capital Gains Effect on Your Future

There are two aspects of the new law that affect retirement planning indirectly but are nevertheless meaningful: the elimination of the capital gains benefit and the effect of lower tax rates on deferred income.

Many companies give their top employees stock and/or allow them to buy the company's stock on some advantageous basis. While not part of any qualified retirement plan, the stock nonetheless often fits into the executive's larger retirement picture.

Commonly, after retirement, by which time the executive has owned the stock for a number of years and seen its value appreciate greatly, he begins to sell it off.

Previously he would enjoy the long-term capital gains benefit on these sales and have 60% of his gain excluded from any taxes. (See Chapters 1 and 2.)

Now, with this benefit eliminated, 100% of his gain will be taxed, and it will be taxed as ordinary income. To be sure, his highest bracket ought to be 28–33%, not 50%, so the loss of the capital gains benefit will not be so painful.

But, from the perspective of a retirement plan, if you are such an executive, and you have been storing up your company's stock with the intention of selling it after retirement, take another look at what the actual value of that stock is likely to be.

Of course, the effect is not limited to stock from your own company. If you have earmarked stock in your portfolio, or any other assets for sale in retirement, review that part of your plan. When it comes time to sell, you will not have the capital gains advantage.

You might also want to do the same recalculation if you were planning to sell your home when you reach retirement, as so many people do. The proceeds from that sale often become a central part of the whole retirement nest egg.

The law still grants you a major benefit on the sale of your principal residence if you are over age 55 and have lived in the house three of the five years before you sell it.

You may exclude $125,000 of your gain from any taxes. Obviously, if your gain is less than that amount, life goes on as before. You take the entire amount tax-free and do as you please with it.

However, if the gain exceeds $125,000, the excess is taxable, unless you invest it in another house. Under the old law the excess was a long-term capital gain of which 60% of the amount over $125,000 was additionally excluded from taxes. But now, if you don't put it into another house, you will be taxed on that excess gain at a maximum rate of 28% if the sale occurred in 1987 and after then at your highest rate, which could be 28–33%.

So, if such a sale has been part of your plan, redo your numbers.

If you have a closely held business, you might be deeply affected by the elimination of the capital gains benefit.

Typically a number of buy-sell agreements between partners, corporate or retirement agreements have been structured around the old laws and the advantages an owner might receive when he terminated his interest in the business. A complete stock redemption by the corporation, for example, gave the owner capital gains treatment on his sale.

Without the capital gains advantage, the results of any such agreements and plans will be radically altered and may no longer serve your needs at all.

Thoroughly review all such agreements with your tax adviser. They may have to be completely redrawn.

Does Deferred Comp Still Make Sense?

Deferred compensation arrangements long have been useful to highly paid executives who could afford to defer some of their compensation.

These are not qualified plans, but deals made between employer and employee, normally available to top executives only.

If your compensation package came to, say, $175,000 a year, and you could afford to defer, say, $25,000, you made such an arrangement with your employer.

Since you did not "constructively" receive that $25,000, you were not taxed on it. Depending on the nature of the agreement, your employer might pay you a specified rate of interest on your deferred funds, say, an interest rate commensurate with seven-year Treasury bills.

When you left the company, you received all of the deferred income plus interest, and your employer would receive a deduction for the amount he paid to you. The whole bundle would be taxed to you at that time as ordinary income, but in theory, since you would then be in retirement, your income would be lower as would your tax bracket.

The catch in the plan was that if your employer went bankrupt, you could find yourself standing in line with all his other creditors trying to collect what he owed you.

The new catch introduced by the TRA is whether it makes sense to defer income if the tax rates are down to 28–33%.

Might it not be better for you to take the income, pay a tax at that rate, and invest the balance? Presumably your return will be greater than the interest your employer would be paying you under the deferred arrangement.

Such a reevaluation is especially valid if you believe as many do that income tax rates are going to rise. In that scenario your tax would be higher some years from now when you receive the deferred income, and you also would have lost the opportunity to invest.

The Key Questions

John Connell, the Touche Ross Tax Partner in Denver and National Director of Personal Financial Management Services, whom we met in Chapters 1 and 2 as he wrestled with the effects of the new law on a client's personal taxes and investments, also develops retirement plans with clients.

One of his keys to successful planning is to pull the whole process out of the realm of the crystal ball. Bring it into reality and reduce it as much as possible to numbers.

Connell starts by distilling the whole futuristic process to a handful of key questions noted at the opening of this chapter. They give focus to the whole effort.

When are you going to retire?

How many years does that give you between now and then to create your retirement financial base?

How much is it going to cost you to live when you retire?

Where is that money going to come from?

So, if you are 45 years old, perhaps you expect to be working for the company or a competitor for another 15 years, 20 years.

That gives you a fair amount of time to build your base, and it is a period that should include your most productive years.

Your salary should be at its highest.

During your last 10 years you should have prime opportunities to invest. Typically, you will be free of most of the financial burdens of your children. If your wife's career had been deterred or limited, she might well now be working full-time again.

This is a critical period, the time when your family's income should be at its peak, your expenses down, and you should then have the opportunity to invest with aggressive regularity. Your investments don't have to be aggressive, but your pattern of investing should be.

It may also be the time to sell the old family home. You don't need four bedrooms anymore. If the market is right, sell it and provide yourself with additional capital to invest.

Look for investments that are going to pay off in your retirement days. You don't need current income. Real estate, even with the limited tax benefits brought by the new law (see Chapter 3), might nevertheless serve your long-term retirement purposes.

Even though that retirement date is 15 to 20 years away, you can project a sense of how much you'll need to live comfortably in retirement.

Where are you going to live?

If you plan to trade your life in the Northeast for another

in the Southwest, your cost of living will drop. All that money spent every winter for heat will be saved. Forget about new winter clothes.

Other living expenses, as noted, should be less as well. No more commuting expenses. Maybe you won't need two cars anymore.

But you will probably be spending more on travel than you do now, and more for health care.

Whether you intend to keep working after your official retirement is doubly meaningful.

First, of course, it should be an additional source of income for those years.

Perhaps more importantly, it should be an additional source of vitality.

Figuring out how you're going to fund these years starts with an appraisal of your current sources of income. Your tax return will give you most of that information, but you'll want to add in any tax-free or tax-exempt income that isn't reflected on the return.

Then it's a matter of looking forward to those next 15 to 20 years. Again, start with taxable income, and adjusting for inflation, perhaps 5% a year, you can estimate your after-tax income, which will also give you an idea of what kind of capital you'll have available for investments. On all these projections, you're better off being conservative. For investments, if you give yourself a 9% pretax return on stocks, 6% pretax on bonds, you should be okay.

In addition, you want to calculate appreciation in existing assets, as well as any other income sources you expect, like inheritances.

Then factor in all of your pension and profit-sharing payments, as well as Social Security benefits; depending on your income limit, half if not all of those benefits may be tax free. Don't overlook any other funds that might become available, like the cash buildup on the investment portion of a single-premium life insurance policy.

With all of that paperwork, the whole picture should become greatly clearer. Among other things you should see whether the numbers match, whether it appears that you will on your present course provide enough to live the way you want in your retirement years.

If there is a gap, adjust the plan. Perhaps you'll have to scale down the way you intend to live. Perhaps you'll decide with your adviser that you'll need to be investing more heavily in the coming years and the money for that will come from cutting back the way you live and spend now. Perhaps you'll try to delay the year you retire. Perhaps you'll end up with a combination of adjustments.

In the end, as advertised, the whole picture will be considerably clearer. And as a result you should dispel some of that natural free-floating anxiety about what lies ahead. But there still is no guarantee, and you still will not be able to control the future.

Their Plan, Your Needs

Indeed, there are so many elements in retirement planning that are not in your control.

To begin with, most people don't have a great deal of choice when it comes to what retirement plan they will have. They go to work for a company, and the company has a plan established. That becomes the individual's primary plan.

There is something of an exception for people who have their own business, as we saw in Chapters 4 and 5. Start your own business, and you have considerably more flexibility in the kind of retirement plans you may provide yourself and your employees.

Indeed, many entrepreneurs who do start their own businesses speak of how deeply important it is for them to have some control over their financial futures. They might have less security than their counterparts with large corporations, but they are happy to make such a trade for the chance to decide, among other profoundly meaningful matters, when they are going to retire, if they are going to retire, and what sort of benefits will be waiting for them.

Sometimes you get the chance to do some shaping of your future even if the company is not your own.

In Phoenix recently, William Raby, the Touche Ross Senior Tax Partner who shepherded the creation of those small, tax-smart business corporations in Chapters 4 and 5, was consulted by Alexander Dysan.

Dysan was in the nice and special position of being wooed and hired by a large national corporation that had taken over an Arizona company, and they wanted him to run it.

Dysan was not going to be able to create a dream retirement package just for himself, Raby told him. Neither the company nor the tax law would permit such special privilege. But he might well be able to enrich his benefits.

The company had a defined contribution plan, sometimes called a *money purchase plan*. Unlike the defined benefit plan, this is not built around a compensation formula and the future projections of an actuary. The one Dysan was being offered was typical. The company would contribute 10% of the compensation of all the employees covered by the plan to a trust each year. The trustees invested the money, and the income was added to the fund and proportionately credited to each participant's account. When Dysan retired, he would receive his proportionate share of the fund.

He'll have a number of options as to how he can receive

the money. A lump-sum payment, put it into an annuity, roll it over into an IRA.

Raby reviewed all the mechanics of the plan with Dysan, whose previous company offered a defined benefit plan as well as some stock option programs for top people. So he was not familiar with the defined contribution plan. That was something Raby frequently encountered. People who were successful in their work who didn't understand the retirement plans of their companies.

Clearing that up is a starting point for Raby. It not only educates his client, but it permits him to examine what the company plan does not offer, what holes exist. After that he can develop a fuller plan to fill the holes.

In comparing the plans of the two companies, Raby found, not to his surprise, that Dysan had overlooked a critical aspect of protection for himself and his family.

With a defined benefit plan, as noted, his benefits were calculated on the expectation that he would receive them until he died. What happens if he leaves the company and dies the following week?

His wife would receive the benefits that would otherwise be going to him. But what if she died soon after him? Or even with him in an accident? Would that substantial fund be paid to their children?

Not unless he made some special provision with the company. Otherwise all those benefits would be lost, even though he had earned them.

Dysan was aghast at the revelation. But Raby had a solution. With many clients who have such plans, he explained, he urges them to negotiate a 10-year certain clause, even if it lowers the amount of the benefits a bit. It guarantees that if the client and his spouse die, the defined benefit will be paid nevertheless for a total of 10 years, the payments usually going to the surviving heirs.

It was too late for Dysan to implant such a protective clause into his old plan.

However, since he was leaving his company before age 65, the retirement age upon which that particular defined benefit plan was based, they had some options.

They could arrange for his former company to make an actuarial calculation of what his benefits would amount to and buy him an annuity plan to cover himself and his wife.

Or they could give him a lump-sum distribution of what was in his plan.

The sum would be transferred from the trustee of that plan directly to the trustee of the plan in his new company.

With those tactics, they would remove the risk that Dysan's benefits would be cut off prematurely. And he would not be taxed on the lump-sum distribution. It would go into the annuity plan or the new qualified plan and continue to grow tax-deferred until he took it out.

One other important suggestion Raby had for Dysan was that he try to get insurance coverage from his new employer that would cover his medical expenses beyond Medicare after he retired.

Though Congress has been debating legislation for such coverage, Dysan would be better off if he could negotiate it with his new company rather than wait for and depend on any federal plan.

This coverage could save him from depleting all or nearly all of his retirement funds if he were struck by a catastrophic illness requiring extended hospitalization and expenses that far outreached Medicare coverage.

This would be a supplement to his other retirement, stock, and profit-sharing plans, and it could be just as significant as the others.

Checklist: Chapter 10

Tax-smart strategies and perspectives for you to consider and discuss with your tax professional:

1. With qualified retirement plans, ones that meet the many requirements of the tax law, your company is entitled to a deduction on any amounts it contributes to such plans. And the funds in the plan are not currently taxed. They will be invested and earn income that is tax-free or tax-deferred until you receive the funds.

2. You may no longer deduct your IRA contribution, unless neither you nor your wife works at a company that offers a qualified plan or your joint adjusted gross income is below $40,000, $25,000 for unmarried individuals. Between $40,000 and $50,000, or between $25,000 and $35,000, the deduction is phased out.

Otherwise you may still contribute up to $2000 to an IRA, $2250 if it's for you and your nonworking spouse, but without any deduction.

The IRA still is allowed to grow on a tax-deferred basis. With your 1987 return you must decide for the first time whether it is better for you to make the contribution or invest it in something like a tax-free bond.

3. You used to be allowed to put 15% of your income or $30,000, whichever was less, into a 401(k) plan and pay no taxes on it. Now the limit is $7000 for the employee contribution. Still, as one of the few remaining ways to "shelter" income, the plan is an especially valuable tax-saving tool.

4. Qualified defined benefit plans are designed to pay you a specified benefit in retirement for as long as you live. The amount of the benefit is tied to a formula based on your compensation from the company. An actuary calculates the data of the plan participants, factoring life expectancies, expected turnover, anticipated compensation in-

creases, and the projected return on the fund's investments. He then tells the employer how much to contribute that year for the fund.

The maximum annual benefit the old law allowed was $90,000, starting at age 62. The new law maintains the $90,000 ceiling, but commencing at age 65. Now at age 62, with a typical plan, you would receive only $72,000.

The previous minimum for retirees at age 55 was $75,000. Today it could be $37,000. At age 60, only $59,000.

There are exceptions for plans in effect by May 6, 1986.

The radical changes require a careful review of such a plan by anyone participating in one.

5. There is now a 15% excise tax on yearly distributions from all your qualified plans that total more than $112,500 or $562,000 with a lump-sum distribution.

There are limited exceptions on plans where the benefits had accrued before August 1, 1986.

6. Ten-year forward averaging has now been cut to five-year averaging. The idea was to provide you with a way to avoid the ruinous taxes you might otherwise face on a lump-sum distribution of a retirement fund that had been growing and growing for many years tax-free. On taking the payout, you then had to pay taxes on it.

However, 10-year forward averaging allowed you to treat a lump-sum distribution from certain qualified plans as if you were receiving the funds over a 10-year period. Obviously that would diminish your taxes, since the assumption was that you had 10 installments rather than one huge one in a single year. You calculated the tax at the rate of a single person paying for that amount of income, times 10 for the 10 years.

The 10-year averaging has now been cut to five-year.

If you reached age 50 by January 1, 1986, you may still elect 10-year based on 1986 tax rates. Or five-year, based on the rates in existence for the year of your distribution.

7. Depending on your circumstances, you might not need or want to take the retirement funds when the plan is scheduled to distribute them.

One alternative, if you get a lump sum is to roll it over into an IRA. Generally, with a rollover, the funds and their earnings will continue to enjoy tax-deferred status.

The IRA rollover might also be used to avoid the new 15% excise tax on excess retirement benefits over $112,500, or $562,500.

Or, if you leave one company for another, you might apply a different sort of rollover. In that case the funds from the first company's plan may be transferred to the plan of the new company with no tax consequences for you, and it would continue to enjoy the special tax-deferred benefits of the plan.

8. The elimination of the capital gains benefit that excluded from taxation 60% of your gain could affect your retirement planning.

If you have company stock that you have been purchasing on a regular basis with a view to selling it during retirement, bear in mind that you will no longer be able to exclude 60% of your gain on the sale of that stock. That could leave a hole in your overall projections.

The same effect pertains to any other stock or asset you have been holding with a retirement sale in mind.

Many people plan to sell their principal residence in retirement, and the anticipated proceeds will figure largely in their financial foundation. If you are over age 55, you may exclude $125,000 of your gain on the sale of your principal residence from any taxes.

The balance is taxable, unless you invest it in another house. Otherwise for 1987 your tax on such excess gain will be 28% maximum and after that at your highest rate, which could be 28–33%. No more 60% capital gains exclusion.

If that sale was central to your retirement calculations, best to redo your numbers.

Closely held business owners could be very much affected by the capital gains change. Typically many of their retirement plans evolve around full redemption of their stock by the corporation, which used to give them a considerable gain at the favored treatment. Today those and other plans may no longer meet projected needs and should be completely reviewed.

9. Deferred compensation arrangements are also to be reexamined because of a change in the new law, the lower income tax rates.

These are not qualified plans, but deals made between employer and employee. They permit an employee to defer a specified amount of his compensation and avoid the tax on it for that year. Depending on the arrangement, the employer will pay the employee some agreed-upon rate of interest on the money and then pay it out when the employee leaves the company, presumably to retire. In theory he will then have less income, so his tax bracket will be lower. So his taxes on the income will be less than they would have been if he had taken it as compensation in those earlier, high-income years.

However, with the lowered tax brackets, the question today is whether it might be wiser for you to forgo such deferred comp arrangements and instead take the compensation and pay the tax at 28–33%, then invest the balance yourself.

Presumably you would be able to generate a higher return than the relatively conservative interest your employer would pay. And if tax rates go up, as many think they will, you will not be faced with a higher tax on that deferred comp when you finally do draw it out.

10. While there is no simple formula for total security in retirement, there are some fundamental questions you can ask to focus your planning:

When are you going to retire? How many years does that give you between now and then to create your financial base for retirement? How much is it going to cost you to live when you retire? Where is that money going to come from?

Your last 10 years of employment become a critical period in fulfilling your retirement needs. You should be at your earning peak during those years with fewer expenses than ever. Investing with aggressive consistency during that period will be essential.

11. You can estimate what it will cost you to live in retirement, factoring in whether you intend to continue earning or not, where you intend to live.

12. Your tax return will show you what your present sources of income are, which you can project forward over the number of years between now and your intended retirement age. Adjust for inflation, for tax-free income, for investment returns, for appreciation in presently owned assets, for any other sources of funds, like inheritances, and be conservative in all those projections.

Add in pension and profit-sharing payments, Social Security benefits.

If the two columns—projected income and projected expenses—don't match, you can adjust your plans. Perhaps scale down your retirement intentions or your present standard of living in order to have more now to invest for those future years. Perhaps you can delay your retirement.

13. If you start your own business, you have considerably more flexibility in deciding what kind of retirement plan you want from your company.

Most people are limited in that they work for a company that has an existing plan, and that's it. Even though your choice might be limited, it is essential that you understand just what your company's plan offers. Only with that clear can you and your adviser fill the holes it leaves.

14. A defined contribution or money purchase plan is offered by many corporations. The company agrees to contribute a specified amount—e.g., 10% of the compensation of all the employees covered by the plan—to a trust each year.

15. If you are participating in a defined benefit plan, try to negotiate a 10-year certain provision. It would require the company to pay your defined benefit for at least 10 years after your benefits commence. Otherwise you might retire, die a week later and your spouse shortly after, and all the benefits you had earned would be lost to your surviving heirs.

16. Try to get your company to provide you insurance as part of your retirement package that covers medical expenses beyond Medicare. Such coverage could save you from being wiped out if you are struck by a catastrophic illness with hospitalization and expenses that far exceed Medicare payments.

Index

AB trust, 172–73, 176
active income, 27, 39–40, 51
alternate minimum tax (AMT), 20–24, 33–34, 61–62
alternative minimum tax income (AMTI), 21
asset freeze, 120, 123, 187, 190
asset transfer, of, 181–82, 189
automobile deduction, 82–83

business-related deductions, 13–15, 31
bypass trust, 170–71, 172–73, 178

capital gains, 8–9, 29, 35–38, 50, 201–3, 213–14
charitable deductions, 22, 24
Clifford trusts, 127–33, 137–39
closely held corporation, 109–22, 123–24
   asset freeze, 112–13, 123, 187, 190
   assets acquired by, 118–19, 124
   capital gains with, 203, 214
   Clifford trust with, 128–30, 138
   disposing of, 112–13, 119–22, 123–24
   estate taxes to, 112–13, 123
   exchange of stock with, 115–16, 123–24
   as family business, 110–11
   flexibility of, 115–16, 124
   going public, 114, 116–18
   holding company for, 188–89
   incentives in, 114, 115–18, 123
   investment plans of, 118–19
   investment transfer to, 48–49, 52
   merging of, 114, 115–18, 123–24
   minority stockholders in, 114, 115–16, 123
   retirement plans with, 207–8, 215
common law marriage laws, 163
consulting business, in retirement, 199–201
consumer credit, interest on, 10–13, 30
corporation (*see also* closely held corporation; S corporation)
   disability deductions by, 87–88, 100
   dividend income of, 90, 101
   earnings invested in, 93–95, 101

corporation *(cont.)*
  limiting liabilities of, 86–87
  medical deductions by, 87, 100
  renting office space to, 96–98, 101
  retirement plans of, 88–93, 100–101
  self-employment compared to, 80–86, 100
Crummey trust (ILIT trust), 159, 170–71, 176

death, sudden, of self and spouse, provision for, 162–63, 176, 209–10
deferred compensation plan, 88–93, 100–101, 203–4, 214
defined benefit plan (money purchase plan), 91–92, 101, 195–97, 208–10, 211–12, 216
defined contribution money purchase plan, 92–93, 101
depreciation deductions, 54–56, 68, 75, 82, 100
disability deductions, 87–88, 100
discriminatory retirement plans, 92–93, 195
dividend income, 17, 32, 90, 101

earnings, investment of, 93–95, 101
education expenses, provision for, 16, 32, 143–45, 154
Employee Stock Ownership Plan (ESOP), 120–22, 124

estate planning *(see also* estate taxes; will), 157–90
  with bonds, 183
  durable power of attorney for, 182–84, 189–90
  flexibility in, 166–67, 177
  gift tax exclusion in, 165–66, 177
  gifts as part of, 181, 185–86
  gross estate value as focus of, 167–68
  holding company with, 188–89
  inflation and, 168–69
  inheritance taxes and, 164
  insurance in, 170–72
  IRS audits and, 185–86
  probate and nonprobate assets in, 161–62
  questions to consider in, 165–67, 177
  transfer of assets in, 181
  trusts in, 170–73, 178, 184–85, 190
  unified credit exemption in, 164, 165, 172, 177, 182, 189
estate taxes *(see also* estate planning)
  for closely held corporation, 112–13, 123
  on jointly purchased property, 135–36, 139
  range of, 158–59, 169–70, 176
excise tax on retirement, 197–98, 200–210, 212

family corporation, *see* closely held corporation

Index

family employees, 82, 100, 109–10, 134, 146, 154–55
family partnership, 146–48, 155
flower bonds, 183
forward averaging, 198–99, 200–201, 212

gift taxes, 131–32
gift tax exclusion
  in estate planning, 165–66, 177, 181, 182, 185–86, 189
  for income shifting, 141–42, 146, 152–53, 154
grantor trust, 127, 137

health club deductions, 14
historic buildings, investing in, 69–71, 78
"hobby losses," 20
holding company, 188–89
home
  income shifting with, 148–53, 155
  refinancing of, *see* refinancing of home
  sale of, in retirement, 202, 213

income, three categories of, 27, 39, 50–51
income averaging, 17–18, 32, 33
income shifting (*see also* Clifford trusts; joint purchase), 125–56
  with children, 140–48, 154–55
  with parents, 148–53, 155
  timing of, 140–43, 153
  TRA effect on, 132–33

insurance
  in estate planning, 170–72, 176
  in retirement plan, 210, 216
interest deductions, TRA effect on, 10–13, 30, 31
intestate laws, effect of, 160–62, 176
investment credits, 69–70, 78
investment goals, 43–44, 50, 51
investment income, 23, 26–27
investment interest deduction, 13, 30–31, 45–49, 52
IRA (Individual Retirement Account),
  rollover maneuver with, 199–210, 213
  rule changes on, 9–10, 26, 29–30, 193–94, 211
irrevocable life insurance trust (ILIT; Crummey trust), 159, 170–71, 176
itemized deductions, 13–15

joint purchase, of property, 134–36, 139

Keogh retirement plan, 85, 91, 100

leverage, 67, 72–74, 76, 78
liabilities, limitation of, 86–87
life estate interest, 135, 139
life insurance, 143–44, 154, 159, 170–72, 176
limited partnership, 27, 47–48, 52
  passive income from, 49, 51, 52–53

maintenance deduction for office in home, 82, 101
malpractice suits, corporation's role in, 87
marital deduction, 159, 163, 173, 176
master limited partnerships (MLPs), 47–48, 52
medical deductions, 15–17, 32
  with corporation, 87, 100
mining, passive losses in, 43–44, 51
minority stockholders, problems with, 114, 115–16, 123
money purchase plan, *see* defined benefit plan
municipal bonds, 44–45

1988, strategic importance of, 29
no-tax mentality, 72–74, 79

office space
  at home, 18–19, 33, 81–83, 100
  purchase of, 147–48, 155
  renting of, 96–98, 101

paper losses, 41–42, 51
partnership, 49, 52–53
passive activity losses (PALs), 72
passive income
  avoidance of, 66
  defined, 27, 39, 51
  generators of (PIGs), 71–72
  from real estate, 60–61, 65–67
  shifting of, 150–52, 156
  tax shelters and, 41–42

tax strategy and, 38–39
passive losses, 20, 23, 41–42
  MLPs and, 47–48
  in real estate, 42
  retirement and, 49
  stock options for avoidance of, 107–8, 123
pension plans, *see* retirement plans
personal exemption, 6–7, 28–29
"phantom stock" agreement, 117–18, 123
political deductions, 17, 32
portfolio income, 27, 39, 51
power of attorney, durable, 182–84, 189–90
professional corporation (p.c.), 84

qualified retirement plans (*see also* defined benefit plans), 91–93, 101, 192–93, 194–95, 211
qualified terminable interest in property (Q-TIP trust), 184–85, 190

rabbi trust, 89–91, 100–101
raw land, investment in, 67–69, 78
real estate, 54–79
  AMT effect on, 23, 26–27, 61–62
  depreciation, 54–56, 68, 75
  investment credits on, 69–71, 78
  joint purchase of, 134–36, 139
  leverage in, 56–57, 67, 72–74, 76, 78

Index

real estate *(cont.)*
  no-tax mentality in, 72–74, 79
  as passive investment, 60–61, 65–67, 71–72, 75–76, 78
  passive losses in, 42, 50, 51
  raw land as, 67–69
  rental/personal proportion in, 65–67, 76–78
  as shelter, 38–39, 41–42, 50, 51
  swap of, 62–64, 76
refinancing of home, 11–12, 16, 22, 30–31, 32
  AMT effect on, 22
  deductibility of interest on, 71, 78
  to fund Clifford trust, 130–31, 138
  investment interest deduction on, 46, 52
  for medical and educational expenses, 16
  return on, 46, 52
  shifting income by, 144–45, 154
remainder interest, 135, 139, 155
rental properties, 42, 51
retirement plans, 191–216
  capital gains and, 201–3, 213–14
  deductions for, 192–93
  defined benefit, 91–92, 101, 195–97, 208–10, 211–12
  discriminatory, 92–93, 195
  estimating future expenses for, 205–7, 215
  excise tax on, 197–98, 200–201, 212
  forward averaging with, 198–99, 200–201, 212
  insurance with, 210, 216
  IRA with, 193–94, 211
  with job switch, 207–10, 215–16
  with own business, 207–8, 215
  qualified, 91–93, 101, 192–93, 194–95, 211
  questions to ask about, 191–92, 204–7, 214–15
  rollover maneuver with, 199–201
  for self-employed, 84–85, 91, 100
  "unqualified," 88–93, 100–101, 203–4, 214
rollover maneuver, 199–210

salary cut to cover deductions, 15, 31
sales tax deductions, 11, 30
savings bonds, 142–43, 154
S corporation, 95–96, 105–8, 122–23
self-employment (unincorporated), benefits of, 81–85, 100
shelters, 38–42, 50–51
special employment contract, 117, 123
special power of appointment, 184, 190
spousal remainder trust (SRT), 131–32, 137–38
standard deduction, 6, 28
start-up capital, 105–8
stock options
  alternatives to, 117

stock options *(cont.)*
  avoiding passive losses with, 107–8, 123
stock sale, after retirement, 201–3, 213

tax brackets, number of, 5, 28
tax-frees, 44–45, 51
tax rates, revised
  effect on AMT, 22–23
  list of, 28
  possible rise of, 8, 29
  table of, 6
Tax Reform Act (TRA), 1–34
ten-year certain clause, 209–10, 216
travel expenses, 13–14, 83
Treasury bonds, long-term, 183
trusts, 170–73, 178, 184–85, 190
two-earner deduction, 17, 32

unearned income, tax rates on, 132–33, 138–39, 140–41, 153–54
unified transfer tax credit
  in estate planning, 164, 165, 172, 177, 182, 189
  in income shifting, 142, 154
"unqualified" retirement plans, 88–93, 100–101, 203–4, 214

Vancouver stock exchange, 116

will *(see also* estate planning; estate taxes)
  cold reading of, 157–58
  disclaimer of, 173–74, 176
  five or five power, 171
  flexibility of, 167
  marital deduction, 159, 163, 173, 176
  need for, 159–63, 176
  nontax matters in, 162–63, 176
  physical location of, 174
  protecting spouse's estate in, 163–64, 172–73, 176–77
  special power of appointment, 184, 190
  sudden death provision, 162–63, 176
  tax-free exemption, 161
  trustee of, 183
  updating, 161–62, 174–75, 176

zero bracket account, 6
zero coupon bonds, 16